Endorsements

D. R. Silva is part of an exciting breed of young authors proclaiming the gospel of radical grace. Unafraid to ask the big questions or confront man-made traditions, he writes so that the church might live up to its full potential in Christ. *How to Overcome Sin* is a book that will challenge the way you think and help you to see your life through the awesome work of the cross.

—Paul Ellis

Author of *The Hyper-Grace Gospel*

D. R. Silva is a great author who navigates the reader around the potholes of religion and leads them into the safe fields of grace.

- Mick Mooney

Author of *SNAP*

D. R. Silva has nailed it again! Every Christian that has been sweating and striving to break free of sin and keep all the rules will truly benefit from reading this book. It's always the knowledge of the Truth that sets us free from slavery to our own misperceptions and personal experience. With wisdom beyond his years, Daniel shares that liberating Truth with ease and simplicity. Let's believe the "too good to be true" Gospel of all that Jesus Christ accomplished for us—and watch our experience rise to meet it!

—Joshua Greeson

Henry Ford famously said "Whether you think you can, or you think you can't - you're right." For years we have been taught in the church, "you are doomed to sin till the day you die." We are taught that God expects us to be holy but our very nature is sinful. This book is a refreshing change, bringing a truth that will be water to your soul — Jesus has made you righteous and completely set you free from sin! The message we choose to embrace determines our experience. Kris Vallotton says "If you believe you are a sinner you will sin by faith." My challenge to you is - read this book - consider what Daniel has to say. You can discover the free gift of righteousness you've been given and that freedom from sin is not nearly as difficult as you think... or you can continue sinning by faith. The choice is yours, choose freedom.

—Phil Drysdale,

PhilDrysdale.com

The second offering from D. R. Silva doesn't disappoint! With practical, easy to understand examples, Daniel walks the reader through his points with clarity and humor. Packed with solid scriptural understanding, this book is a must read for anyone who has ever thought "Why can't I stop doing that?!"

—Rebecca Clayton

Daddy's House Trust
www.daddyshouse.org.uk

How To Overcome Sin by D. R. Silva proves that a book doesn't have to be a few hundred pages in length to make a powerful impact on the reader. The first half is a slow burn, laying the proper theological groundwork, and the second half crackles like a firework. Without even the slightest hint of arrogance, Silva fearlessly confronts some of Christianity's biggest, joy-robbing giants. Prepare yourself for a challenging, authentic experience—you're guaranteed to walk away with a head full of knowledge, a smile on your face and a renewed sense of hope.

—Sarah Dunsworth

Sarah Dunsworth Ministries

How to Overcome Sin

A PRACTICAL GUIDE TO FREEDOM

D. R. Silva

Up-Arrow Publishing
Havre, Montana

Contents

To the hopeless

*"In the past you were full of darkness
but now you are full of light in the Lord.
So live like children who belong to the light."*

—EPHESIANS 5:8 (ERV)

Preface

When scripture calls us free from the Law of sin and death, it really means we're free indeed. That may sound like an obvious statement, but as much as people proudly proclaim those kinds of things, many still hold onto spiritually-disguised excuses that diminish how true they are. Some make it sound as if we're only figuratively free, others say we are only "positionally" free, and a large majority believes that we won't *literally* be free from sin until we get to heaven.

I myself used to believe and preach those things. I expected to sin every day until I died, and my daily actions proved how right I was. But even though I believed I would always sin, I still felt the intense pressure of the Christian standard to try my hardest to avoid it. Even though my leaders emphasized how wicked and sinful we are, they simultaneously demanded that we all better try our hardest not to sin. Like bringing an exercise bike to the Olympics, there was a goal I knew I had to aim for, but no matter how hard I pedaled I always found the same result: absolute exhaustion and zero forward progress.

I struggled with depression and suicidal thoughts for years, caused by the constant disappointment of failing to avoid the things I knew I could never avoid. But now I live in peace, thankful to know that through the death and resurrection of Jesus we're *completely* free from sin, here in this life, right now in this moment. It's not a figurative freedom, or a freedom that will only be available if we endure the suffering of the exercise bike long enough. Instead, as the ministry of Jesus has shown us, it's God's will for us to be free from all sin, sickness, death, and every bad fruit that sin brought to us, here in this life.

It's okay if you disagree—I don't plan to pull any funny tricks to coerce you into accepting these things—but I do hope to give you something truly amazing to think about.

✳✳✳

One of the major reasons sin thrives in the lives of Christians is because we've indirectly convinced ourselves that it's supposed to. Although many sermons are full of demands to quit sinning, they are followed up (or prefaced) with prayers about how sinful we really are. If we believe we are only "sinners saved by grace" then are we so surprised when we do what "sinners" do? Although some of our worship songs and sermons are filled with amazing truths about freedom, many others contradict them by telling us that we aren't really free. Although it's never said directly, it's often implied, when in one breath we're free from sin, but in the next we're prone to it. How are you supposed to avoid sin if you're constantly given the idea that you *want* to do it? Yes, you *shouldn't* want to do it, but you *do want* to do it because your heart is wicked. Peter warned that it's these double-minded doctrines that cause us to be blown back and forth by the wind.

Instead of preaching the *complete* freedom from sin that scripture preaches, we've watered down Christ's work concerning sin to one magnificent point: Forgiveness. Yes, He died on the cross and went through the gauntlet of brutality to forgive our sins, but we're still stuck in sinful bodies with a sinful nature until He raptures us or we die (whichever comes first).

Don't misunderstand me. Forgiveness is great! But with that kind of logic we're not truly free, we're only waiting for a freedom that He has yet to bring (and one that can only be attained through physical death). With that logic, no matter how forgiven we are, we can never stop doing the things we keep needing forgiveness for, which keeps us in the same spiritual hell we were in before we called on Him to save us.

That's a frustrating conclusion. On one hand God is demanding that you stop sinning, but on the other, you can never stop sinning because it's in your nature. Yet, even though God knows it's in your nature and you can't avoid it, He still expects you to try your hardest to. If you've been down that rabbit hole as far as I have, you know how much it feels like you're constantly being torn in two (insert the "dual natures" idea that we will deal with shortly).

✳✳✳

I've encountered so many people who are as messed up as I was. The internet is full of prayer groups where people ask for help with sin they don't think they can ever overcome. They don't know that real answers for these problems exist. Instead, many have accepted that this is just what we've been handed: a lifetime struggle with a sin disease we never asked for or did anything to deserve. I've been there. Those were the darkest days of my whole life (even worse than before I became a Christian!).

As much as I sang songs about chains being broken and said "amen" to all the scriptures about being free from sin, I was still attached to my sin by a ball-and-chain the size of my ego. As much as I sang about being free, I was imprisoned by my own performance. I couldn't let go of the idea that it was up to me to try harder and pedal faster if I wanted things to change. And when things didn't change, I was made to feel like I wasn't trying hard enough, so I felt an even greater obligation to try even harder and pedal even faster. On it and on it goes: the perpetual circle of self-focus and condemnation.

The issue was never that I wasn't trying hard enough, or that I wasn't sincere enough about my devotion to God, but that I was sitting on something that was never designed to move anybody forward (that metaphorical exercise bike).

It took a while before I could admit those things to myself. Our obsessive need to pretend we have faith is what keeps us from actually having it. We'd rather pretend to have it all together by the appearance of being good rule keepers and Bible experts, than to admit that we're desperately lacking real answers like everybody else. But when I finally was honest with myself about my lack of answers, that's when I became motivated to go and find those answers on my own. I became unsatisfied with the stock answers Christians kept offering me, so I went out to find answers that actually worked.

"You just need to spend more time in the Word, brother!"

"You just need to pray more, brother!"

"You just need to come to church more, brother!"

"Have you tithed this week, brother?"

No! I don't want to be told to try harder. I've already tried that! Give me REAL answers that will help me out of this hole I'm in!

If you're reading this book, odds are you're looking for real answers, too. I'll tell you up-front that this book isn't a 12 step program on how to avoid sin. I considered writing it like a typical "how to" book, but I think the church has enough programs aimed at fixing people's behavior. The problem isn't that we don't have enough methods and formulas for good behavior (we have plenty), but that none of those programs or formulas are designed to change our heart, which is often where the source of the problem is. Many of the programs we've created are only designed to change our behavior and outside appearances through strict disciplines and willpower, despite the sin we believe is in our heart.

This book is focused on heart change, what Jesus called "cleaning the inside of the cup." It's through heart change that our actions will change naturally without the burden of force or the stress of trying to fulfill impossible obligations.

✳✳✳

I've been in full-time-ministry mode since I was 16-years-old. I've been around a lot of Christians throughout my life. I know the secret misery expressed behind closed doors. I know the sly Sunday smile that hides the tears and frustration we have Monday through Saturday. I know how it is to talk about the "joy of the Lord" but be trapped in a sorrow beyond words. I know how it is to say things like, "Jesus is my life," while spending most nights fantasizing about never waking up the next morning. Best of all, I know how it is to spiritualize all of these things with out-of-context Bible verses to make them easier to cope with.

I wrote this book, not because I have a desire to force my opinion or present myself as an expert theologian, but because I've found answers to problems I was told there are no answers to until death. I remember where I've come from, and I know that many more are still there.

I wrote this book because I love the church and every individual in it, and I want to see her living up to her full potential in Him. I want every Christian on the planet to know that we were made to move "from glory to glory" not from sin to sin.

While I have plenty to say on the subject of the Law and the sin nature, I've purposely decided to keep this book as short and simple as possible to avoid overwhelming anyone. I've tried to address as many important points as I can, while also considering some of the common questions that are asked in response. But I may not have addressed *every* point or question, so if you'd like to read more on this subject, please visit my blog, SaintsNotSinners.org, where you'll find many more encouraging articles on this subject and others.

Please note that I don't approach this subject as an expert theologian, but as a lifelong Christian who has many questions. If you're looking for a professionally polished sermon from a formally educated religious expert, you might find yourself disappointed by my informality. However, I've done my studies and I've found answers that many of the experts never seem to offer. My overall goal with anything I write is not only to provide answers, but to provoke questions and give you a head start on finding answers for yourself.

This book was written with an undying love and passion for the saints.

D. R. Silva

March 2014

The Romans 7 Paradox

For my first six years as a Christian, I was trapped in a sin and depression I couldn't bear. I was bouncing back and forth from one disappointing relationship to another, desperate to find a place of acceptance and belonging. Worse yet, in the relationships that actually stood a chance, I found myself uncontrollably manipulating the person I cared about the most. In one breath I would say, "I love you and I want to marry you," and in the next I would use her trust to coerce her into sending me topless pictures, taking advantage of my previous promise and reassuring her, "We're getting married anyway. It's not like I won't see you that way eventually!" To my continuous disappointment, I seemed to hurt and manipulate the people I loved the most; I became an expert at it.

As a result, I had a very deep hatred for myself, and I lived in a state of constant regret and guilt. I had no fix for the problems I was facing, and I had nobody to talk to about any of them because of all the shame I felt. I knew how much God wanted me to do good, but I also believed that I could never carry it out. The more I hurt the person I loved, the more convinced I became that I truly did have a wicked heart. The more convinced I became that my heart was wicked, the more wicked I seemed to behave.

One night, in pure frustration, I screamed at God in the darkness of my room. "What is the point of being a Christian if I have to try my hardest to keep these rules that I can never keep? If this is the Christian life then I don't want to be a Christian anymore! I might as well go do the sin I'm going to end up doing anyway and just get it over with!" I didn't know if my tone would offend Him, but I didn't care. In my mind, the best response He could have given was getting angry and dropping a bolt of lightning on my head.

After realizing (and believing) that I was prone to sin for the rest of my life, I just wanted my life to be over with as quickly as possible. Whether or not I went to hell after I died was far from my mind; as far as I was concerned, I was already there. I was twenty-years old when I prayed that. The thought of spending another sixty or more years in the struggle I was in didn't sound very appealing. The idea that I would continue ruining relationships with bratty temper tantrums, guilt-trips and manipulation terrified me. I felt trapped in a life I didn't want to be in.

While many of my Christian friends and pastors would say that sinning is our nature (in other words, it's natural for us to gravitate towards it), they would also say that we have to keep fighting it. Although they believe we can never stop sinning until we die, it's our responsibility to try our hardest to avoid sin as long as we're alive. But what's the point of fighting something you know you can never defeat? All we will do is tire ourselves out in a hopeless battle.

Many today will say that the things in this book are a "license to sin," but for me, there was no greater license to sin than being told it was my nature to do it. In believing that it was my nature, I reached a point where I thought that it would just be better to get it over with whenever I was tempted, since no matter how much I fought, I would always end up losing to sin eventually anyway. Why should I fight and struggle to get out of quicksand, when no matter how much I fight and struggle it's going to overtake and kill me? Why should I torture myself by delaying the inevitable, knowing there's no escape? Let's just make it quick and painless, so I can move on! That's how I began thinking.

My life sounded a lot like Romans 7, the chapter many Christians use to defend the normality of continuous sin. The thinking goes like this: *If Paul so clearly struggled with a sin nature after becoming a Christian then it's perfectly normal for us to struggle with it, too!*

I hope the rest of this chapter [and book] gives you a more hopeful perspective.

Who's Paul Talking To?

If you read the context of Romans 7, Paul is speaking of those who are bound to the Law, (those who try really hard to live up to all the rules), not to those who have been freed from the Law by grace. If you read the first verse in Romans 7, he says that he's now talking to those who are familiar with the Law.

Why does he suddenly make this distinction in the middle of his letter? Because those who are familiar with the Law are going understand exactly what he's about to say. They will read "I do not do the good I want to do" and immediately think, "Oh goodness. I know exactly what that's like!"

"Do you not know, brothers and sisters—for I am speaking to those who know the Law—that the Law has authority over someone only as long as that person lives?" – Romans 7:1 (NIV)

Indeed, many today read Romans 7 and say, "I know exactly what that's like!" But then they conclude that Paul must be saying that sin is the believer's destiny. As long as they are alive they will be caught in the middle of a battle between good and evil, both of which live in and struggle for control of the same body (yours).

However, in Romans 6 Paul is talking about people under grace, who are free from the Law. As you'll see in the table on the next page, if Paul were talking about his current situation in Romans 7, then he completely contradicted everything he had just told them in Romans 6.

Romans 6 (NIV)	Romans 7 (NIV)
Dead to Sin:	**Alive to Sin:**
"We are those who have died to sin; how can we live in it any longer?" (6:2)	"As it is, it is no longer I myself who do it, but it is sin living in me." (7:17-18)
"...our old self was crucified with him so that the body ruled by sin might be done away with." (6:6)	"...Now if I do what I do not want to do, it is no longer I who do it, but it is sin living in me that does it." (7:19-20)
"...because anyone who has died has been set free from sin." (6:8)	"What a wretched man I am! Who will rescue me from this body that is subject to death?" (7:24)
"...count yourselves dead to sin but alive to God in Christ Jesus." (6:10-11)	
Not Slaves to Sin:	**Still Slaves to Sin:**
"For we know that our old self was crucified with him so that the body ruled by sin might be done away with, that we should no longer be slaves to sin..." (6:7)	"We know that the Law is spiritual; but I am unspiritual, sold as a slave to sin." (7:14)
"For sin shall no longer be your master, because you are not under the Law, but under grace." (6:14)	"For what I want to do I do not do, but what I hate I do." (7:15)
"...though you used to be slaves to sin...You have been set free from sin and have become slaves to righteousness." (6:17-18)	"...Although I want to do good, evil is right there with me. For in my inner being I delight in God's Law; but I see another Law at work in me... making me a prisoner of the Law of sin at work within me..." (7:21-24)
"But now that you have been set free from sin..." (6:22)	"I myself in my mind am a slave to God's law, but in my sinful nature a slave to the law of sin." (7:25)

So which is it, Paul? Are we free or not? Some will say it's a paradox, but really it's nothing more than a blatant contradiction if the popular interpretation is true. How can Paul be free from sin in Romans 6, saying that the old body of sin has been done away with, but then turn right around in Romans 7 and say that he's still enslaved to sin in his body? How confusing would that have been to his original audience who didn't have verses and chapters to pick and pull from, and would have had to read the letter straight through?

If you read the book of Romans as a whole like his original audience did, not just Romans 7 as an individual chapter, or the individual verses as individual statements, you'll see that Romans 7 is only emphasizing what he said in the previous two chapters (Romans 5 and 6), and setting up for the exciting news in the next chapter (Romans 8).

> "For sin shall no longer be your master, because you are not under the Law, but under grace." - Romans 6:14 (NIV)

What is Romans 7 about? It's all about a man who is still under Law, and therefore still mastered by sin. He's telling them what it's like to be under the Law, and how the Law increases sin.[1] He's not talking about the new man under grace who has been set free from sin, but the old man under Law, who, through the Law, is still ruled by sin.

The main point of Romans 6 is that, just as Christ died to sin once for all, we too are to consider ourselves dead to sin, *once for all.*[2] So how can we go from that, directly to Romans 7 and say, "I'm still alive to sin! It lives in my body and controls my actions!" If sin still controls my actions then I'm lying when I say I'm no longer its slave, because a slave is someone whose actions are controlled by another.

You're dead to sin *because* you're free from the Law. If you think of yourself as dead to sin but continue trying to live up to the Law, then just as Paul said in Romans 7:8-9, sin will spring to life. The result is that you will feel like a Romans 7 man (you want to do good and obey the Law, but it never works out), even though you're a Romans 6 man (no longer sin's slave).

Paul's Analogy

If a slave dies, how hard do they have to try to resist the commands of their former master? Not very hard, they're dead. Likewise, though you were once a slave to sin and had no choice in obeying your master, that slave-self has died and that master has no more power over you. In death you have been freed from his control.

Whereas before, when your master would command you to do something and you would automatically obey, now you have a choice because sin is no longer your master, therefore it can no longer tell you what to do. Although you still have the ability to say "Yes!" to sin's command, you have the right and the power to say, "No!"

The Wages of Sin

Romans 6:23 says, "The wages of sin is death, but the gift of God is eternal life." It's a popular verse, and it's often yanked out of context, half-quoted and plastered to picket signs to scare college kids into "getting right with God." But the context of the verse isn't even about "sinners" getting saved, it's about the Christians who already are.

Wages are something you work for, something you earn by fulfilling another person's commands. You were once a slave to sin and your payroll check was paid out in death, but "the gift of God is eternal life." What is a gift? It's something you don't earn and you don't have to work for—the opposite of wages. Again, you were once ruled by sin, and you received death for your labor, but now you have been set free from sin and you receive the gift of eternal life through the labor of Christ.

It's a way better deal, don't you think?

Your New Master

Sin was the master of the old you who was under the Law (and because you were under the Law, you were mastered by sin), but that person died. The new you under grace is alive to God in Christ.

What does Paul follow the dead slave analogy up by saying? You're now slaves to God, and slaves to righteousness! Does that mean you're literally God's slave and He's standing over you with a whip, forcing you to do hard labor for Him? No. Paul said he was only using the analogy of slavery because of the simple human terms his readers could understand.[3] It was a parable. Remember that Jesus said, "My yoke is easy and my burden is light," and "You're not my slaves, you're my friends."[4]

The point Paul was making with the analogy is that just as it was easy to yield our bodies to the work of sin when it was our master, now we can just as easily yield our bodies to carry out God's righteous work because He is (remember, it's a metaphor) our new master.

Married With Children

To push the point further, in Romans 7 Paul makes the comparison to a husband and wife. He says that as long as the husband is alive, the wife is bound to him by Law, but if the husband dies, she is released from the Law and is able to unite herself to another. What point is he making? You used to be in a covenant relationship with the Law, but the old husband died and now you're free to marry another (namely, Jesus).[5] Why is that important to understand? Read the rest of Romans 7. Paul tells us exactly what happens in your marriage to the Law.

There's a reason Moses died in the wilderness and wasn't allowed to go into the Promised Land. He was the representative of the Law, and it was to show (as a sort of prophecy) that you can't reach the Promised Land through the Law, neither can you take the Law with you into the Promised Land. In fact, you can't reach the Promised Land at all unless the Law dies! Who was Joshua? He was a representative (a shadow) of the future Christ.

Jesus = Yeshua = Joshua

In the same way that Moses' death was a type and shadow of the future, Joshua leading the people into the Promised Land was a type and shadow of Christ (Yeshua) leading people into the Promised Land apart from the Law (leaving the dead body of Moses behind).

Now, although the Law itself is holy, righteous and good, sin took advantage of the Law and used it to reproduce more sin. Paul says this clearly in Romans 7, verses 8 and 9:

"...apart from the Law, sin is dead. Once I was alive apart from the Law; but when the Law came, sin sprang to life and I died."

Again in Romans 5:20:

"The Law came to increase sin..."

Why does sin increase? Because of the Law. What happens when your life revolves around the Law? Sin increases. So is the remedy to sin being stricter enforcers of the Law? No. That's what makes sin worse. Still don't believe me? He says it again in 2 Cor. 15:56.

"The strength of sin is the Law."

What does he mean by that? The Law is to sin what spinach is to Popeye. Do you want an easier time living free from sin? Stop giving spinach to Popeye!

It starts by separating yourself from the commands of the Law. It's that old dead husband that causes sin to spring to life, and when sin springs to life all it wants to do is use the Law to multiply. But you aren't committed to that husband anymore, now you are free to unite yourself with another. Since you've been united to a new Husband who is fully alive, why would you ever want to cheat on Him by running back to the old dead one?[6]

The old legalistic husband, who attracted the seduction of sin with his rules and regulations, is dead. Now you have been freed from your commitment to him, and have been united to a new husband who *repels* the seduction of sin with His kindness and grace.

It's important for us to understand these things if we're to truly begin living free from sin. In order to get free from the perpetual machine, you first have to know how it operates and what fuels it.[7]

Faith in Works

Why does the Law attract sin? Because it makes it all about you and what you do, instead of Him and what He did. The Law says, "You must do these things to get this reward! You must keep these rules to keep God happy!" And although none of us ever intentionally become self-righteousness and prideful, the Law brings that out of us because it creates a competition between us and our brothers. It causes us to say, "I obeyed more rules than Daniel, therefore I deserve more favor from God!" or even worse, "They didn't obey enough rules, therefore they deserve God's judgment!"

One only needs to look at the Pharisees to see what kind of abuse this turns into. Their self-worth was so attached to their own work and effort to please God and impress man that it led them to murder anyone who offered God's love and forgiveness for free (including God's own son). Even today, it's easy to become prideful and boastful about our own work when we have this long checklist of things we can rub in other people's faces, making ourselves look and feel more superior and self-important than those who don't obey as many rules as we do.

A Level Playing Field

Grace is different than Law. It declares us as equals no matter what we do (and consequently it becomes offensive to those who base their lives on "doing"). It doesn't matter if you start work early or get there an hour before the doors close, we all get the same pay, and none of us has the right to complain about it because it's coming out of His pocket and He can do whatever He wants to do with His own money.[8]

The idea of living without the Law offends many because they don't know what else to measure their worth and goodness by besides their own hard labor. They don't trust themselves or other people to behave right without a rigid set of instructions that tell them how to behave. Good Christians are judged by how hard they work to keep the Ten Commandments, go to Church on time every Sunday, or have a successful ministry. But God says, "You're good because I made you good!" Grace says, "Your work is appreciated, but it isn't required. You can never earn what I give away for free!" That makes a lot of people upset because it diminishes the thing they've spent their whole life trying to earn, and the thing they've put their trust in: their own effort to make themselves good enough.

When God created Adam, how much work did Adam do before God "looked at what He created and said, 'it is good.'"? Adam hadn't done anything yet, but he was good because God made Him good. When Jesus got baptized, how successful was His ministry before God said, "This is my son with whom I am well pleased"? It wasn't successful. In fact, it hadn't even begun. Jesus hadn't preached a single sermon or worked a single miracle, but still God was pleased. Why? Because "this is my son."

It's who you are not what you do that pleases God and makes Him happy with you.

Before I heard this gospel I didn't know how to comprehend my worth apart from my works. I constantly had to be *doing*, or at least having the *will to do*, otherwise I was a "bad Christian" who disappointed God. I never would have thought that the way to improve my behavior was to *stop* trying to improve my behavior! Goodness, that sounds so backwards, doesn't it?

You might be thinking, "Okay, but how am I supposed to live a moral and godly life without the commands of the Law?" It's simple: "The grace of God has come... it teaches us to say 'No!' to ungodliness."[9] It's relationship with Jesus, not Moses (Grace, not Law) that reduces the sin in our life. Not because we try hard not to sin, but because our heart is so changed by His grace and kindness that we cannot continue sinning. We reckon ourselves dead and let Him live His life through our body.

Although the Law tells you what not to do, it never empowers you to not do it. Grace on the other hand, teaches us to say "no," and then empowers us to follow through. Because where the Law is based on the power and will of the flesh, grace is based on the power and will of the Spirit. Where the flesh is weak, the Spirit is willing.

Flesh vs. Spirit

In the flesh (that is, the sinful nature) I can will my mind to do good, but I can never will my actions. In the Spirit, my mind and actions are willed to do good naturally, because the Spirit in me is good, and it is living through my body.

> "I know that good does not dwell in me, that is, in my flesh. For the will to do good is there, but the ability to carry it out is not." – Romans 7:18 (Personal Paraphrase)

People often pull that verse and the ones following out of context and say, "See! Nothing good dwells in me!" *Ah!* But look at it again. "Good does not dwell in me, *that is, in my flesh.*"[10]

> "You, however, are not in the flesh but in the Spirit, if in fact the Spirit of God dwells in you." – Romans 8:9 (NIV)

You are no longer in the weak-willed flesh, but in the strong-willed Spirit. What is the will of the flesh? It's pride and selfishness; it's self-righteousness. It's entirely based on what you can see, touch, taste and feel. It's the idea that "I can do this if I just will myself hard enough!" It's the corrupt mindset that says, "I can attain life apart from the Life Source!"

It's not that God is cocky and doesn't want anyone to be independent, it's that independence is self-destructive because the labor given to the goal of attaining eternal life through our behavior will exhaust us to the point of death every time (if not physically, then spiritually). The sinful flesh makes it all about *you* and *your* ability to carry out the commands of the Law in order to be "good enough" and make God happy.

To live by the Spirit is to let the Spirit live through you. It's *His* will and *His* ability operating through you, so you are free to find rest as you let His will naturally take place through your life. That's what it means to say, "I no longer live, Christ lives in me. The life I live in the body I live by faith in the Son of God who loved me and gave Himself for me."[11]

How do you begin living by the Spirit? You start by abandoning your determination to obey the Law. You throw your hands in the air, surrender and admit to yourself, "I can't do this. No matter how hard I try, this is absolutely impossible!"

I know it sounds heretical at first. The Law has been hammered into our head every Sunday since we started going to Church, but how well has that worked out for the Church so far? How free are we really? If we were really free, we wouldn't have so many excuses for why we will never stop sinning until we get to heaven.

Faith in Christ

"What a wretched man I am! Who will rescue me from this body that is subject to death?" – Romans 7:24 (NIV)

Who was the wretched man? It was the man trapped under Law and controlled by sin. The man so wrapped up in his own flesh efforts that all he could see was how wicked and hopeless he was. That man could never carry out the good he wanted to do, and to his continuous disappointment he always did the bad things he didn't want to do. Sound familiar?

That was my life for a long time. Many Christians still live that way, using Romans 7 as their justification when Romans 7 was never about Christians in the first place!

What's the answer, then? Who will rescue that wretched man from the body of death?

"Thanks be to God, who delivers me through Jesus Christ our Lord!" –
Romans 7:25 (NIV)

Jesus delivered us from the body of death that was hopelessly
united to the Law that enabled sin through the weak will of the
flesh. What's the conclusion?

*"Therefore, there is now no condemnation for those who are in Christ Jesus,
because through Christ Jesus the Law of the Spirit who gives life has set you
free from the Law of sin and death." – Romans 8:1-2 (NIV)*

Do you see it? "Through Christ Jesus." He's the one who
delivered you from the body of death, and the one who set you free
from the Law of sin and death. It's not up to you to try harder, it's up
to you to believe that what He did was good enough.

What is the Law of sin and death? It's the thing Paul was just
talking about all throughout Romans 7. The will to do good, but the
powerlessness to carry it out—the never ending circle of self-
centeredness that leads to self-condemnation and becomes eternal
death.[12]

It's not about you trying to set yourself free from sin through
your own will-power, but about trusting that His work has already
set you free. Jesus already did everything that needed to be done.

*"For what the Law was powerless to do because it was weakened by the flesh,
God did by sending His son..." – Romans 8:3 (NIV)*

The Law was powerless to set us free and remove our
condemnation because it was based entirely on our ability in the
flesh. Who fixed the problem? God did. How did He do it? By
sending Jesus. Why did He send Jesus?

> *"...in order that the righteous requirement of the Law might be fully met in us, who do not live according to the flesh but according to the Spirit." –* Romans 8:4 (NIV)

You already met the righteous requirement of the Law, and you did absolutely nothing in your own effort to achieve that goal! Isn't that exciting? Christ did it all on your behalf. The obvious question is *why are so many people still trying to do what Christ has already done?*

Off the Hook

Since the requirements of the Law have already been fully met in us, are we to continue trying to meet them on our own? Many will give a resounding "yes!", but think about that for a second, how much sense does it actually make?

If through a contract I'm in a committed relationship with my phone company, how silly would it be if after I fulfilled the obligations of that 2-year commitment, I continued sending them money every month for the rest of my life? Wouldn't that be a pointless endeavor? Indeed it would. So it is to try and fulfill the Laws of the old covenant. That contract was fulfilled, which means you've been released from it, which means you're now free to move on to a better company with a better plan.[13]

> "But see, brother, there is a difference between a contract and a covenant."

Indeed there is! If I want to get out of the contract with my phone company early, I have to pay a monetary fine; if I want to get out of a covenant, the fine I pay is my life. Incidentally, Romans 6 says that the old man who was in a covenant with God—the one established in the Old Testament through Moses—died with Christ on the cross. Therefore we have been let off the hook from that covenant and are no longer under its obligations. We aren't bound to it until death because we already died, and we were raised to new life with Christ under a covenant established on His ability, not ours.

Now many will say, "I agree that we're under grace, not under Law, but I still think we need to obey the Law!" Many who say that will also say, "There needs to be a balance of grace and Law!" Is it true? Is there some mystical balance between grace and Law? Although we're in the new covenant should we still try to live by the standards of the old, at least to some degree?

In the next chapter, we'll examine what scripture says about that.

Endnotes

[1] See Romans 5:20, "The law came that sin might increase..."

[2] See Rom. 6:10-11. "Just as He died to sin once for all... in the same (once for all) way, consider yourselves dead to sin, but alive to God in Christ. How can people say they consider themselves dead to sin when sin is all that's talked about by most Christians?

[3] See Rom. 6:19

[4] See John 15:15

[5] A covenant relationship is one that is in place until one of the parties dies. As long as both in the agreement are alive, the covenant stands. But if one party dies, the other is off the hook and is no longer bound by the agreement.

[6] See 1 Cor. 6:17

[7] Now, if you've never been fed the religious obligations of upholding the Law, you're already in a good position. For my first 3 months as a Christian, I was oblivious to any Christian obligations and rules, so all I spent my time doing was enjoying communion with God. 24 hours a day, even in my sleep, I was in constant communion with Him. It wasn't until I was introduced to the Law (the religious demands that I was "required" to uphold to keep a "healthy relationship" with God), that everything began to spiral downward and out of control. I'm sure many of you would find something similar if you trace the problem back to where it first began.

[8] See Matt. 20:1-16

[9] See Titus 2:11-12

[10] Some translations replace "flesh" with "sinful nature."

[11] See Galatians 2:20

[12] See James 1:15

[13] See Heb. 8:6-13

The Mystical Balance of Grace and Law

There have been many times when I've talked with people about the things in this book and they respond by saying, "You're right, brother. But we have to have balance." *Cringe.* For a while, "balance" was like the Christian "B word" for me. It was like that scene in The Lion King where one of the Hyenas kept saying, "Mufasa, Mufasa, Mufasa!" and the other one would just shudder.

Don't get me wrong, I have nothing against the idea of balance. But the way people often use the word is like a "get out of jail free" card. It's said in a way that avoids addressing the points and scriptures at hand, and instead of the person admitting that those points are worth consideration, they just find a clever way to wiggle out of it and avoid it altogether while still maintaining an appearance of spirituality and not-wrongness. It's religious pride disguised as spirituality.

Don't misunderstand me. When it comes to life and Christianity, there are numerous things that require balance. But when it comes to Law and Grace, there is no balance, there's only one or the other. Scripture says this over and over. And although God's grace isn't thwarted by the Law, a person's ability to receive His grace is, because they are so wrapped up in making offerings to Him that they don't even see the offering He has made to them.

How to Fall from God's Grace

Have you ever heard the term "fall from God's grace"? Oftentimes when it's used, what the person means is that someone has turned from God's commandments and returned to a life of sin. If you live in the States, you may more often hear people say it about America as a whole.

> "We have turned our backs on God's holy Law! We have fallen from God's grace! Now we are suffering His wrath and judgment!"

It's usually accompanied by another popular saying, "Your sin separates you from God!" Both of these beliefs of falling from God's grace are associated with the amount of sin you do, but funny enough, the opposite is true! Scripture doesn't say that backsliding (or falling from God's grace) comes from turning your back on the Law, but rather, it comes from turning your attention *towards* the Law! Cringe-worthy to hear at first, I know, but let's look at the verses because Paul made it clear.

> *"For if you are trying to make yourselves right with God by keeping the Law, you have been cut off from Christ! You have fallen away from God's grace." – Galatians 5:4 (NLT)*

"Yeah, but the NLT isn't very trustworthy!"

No? Then let's look at everybody's favorite version, the KJV.

"Christ is become of no effect unto you, whosoever of you are justified by the Law; ye are fallen from grace."

How about the NASB?

"You have been severed from Christ, you who are seeking to be justified by Law; you have fallen from grace."

NIV?

"You who are trying to be justified by the Law have been alienated from Christ; you have fallen away from grace."

They all make the same point: if you are trying to get (or stay) right with God by keeping the commands of the Law, you have fallen from grace and have been separated from Christ.

Now, before we continue let me say that I don't believe this is speaking of a *physical* or *spiritual* separation from Christ, but a mental one. Paul said we are *one spirit* with Christ, so who can separate us? None. But in returning to the self-righteousness of Law keeping, we are once again rejecting the righteousness that only comes to us through faith in Christ. In our hearts and minds we are separating ourselves from Christ and His work, and are therefore falling from the benefits of His grace. Galatians 5:4 isn't about Christians who went back to a life of sin, it's about Christians who went back to a life of Law-keeping.

Do you see what I mean when I say you can't have a perfect balance of Law and Grace? To have Grace is to fall from Law; to have Law is to fall from Grace. You can only have one or the other, not both. It's as black and white as the pages of this book.

Why Sin Thrives Under the Law

"But their minds were closed. And even today, when those people read the writings of the old agreement, that same covering hides the meaning. That covering has not been removed for them. It is taken away only through Christ. Yes, even today, when they read the Law of Moses, there is a covering over their minds." – 2 Cor. 3:14-15 (ERV)

Is it the Law itself that blinds you to Jesus? Not technically. But sin, using the Law to its own advantage blinds you to Christ because it forces you to look at yourself and your own works over Christ and His works. It causes you to compare yourself and your goodness to other people, rather than comparing yourself to Him. That is, after all, the point of the Law, which is why Jesus even preached it. But His version of the Law wasn't the watered-down version the religious leaders were preaching. His Law was preached in the full severity it was meant to be preached in.

See, the religious leaders of Jesus' day had made the Law doable, and thus deceived themselves into thinking they could fulfill it by their own efforts and gain favor with God.

They said, "Oh. Don't have sex with a married woman? Easy!"[1]

But Jesus said, "No. If you even *think* about it in your heart, you've done it."

They said, "Don't murder? Easy!"[2]

But Jesus said, "No. If you even call someone a 'fool', you're in danger of hell fire."

Was He enforcing the Law to encourage us and say, "You can do it! I've come to show you how!" No. He was preaching the Law as it was meant to be preached in the first place: in a way that would make you so hopeless and distraught at your own ability to carry it out and lift such a heavy burden, that you're only possible response could be, "God, help me." We see this with the rich young ruler.[3]

The Law was never meant to give us confidence that we could obey it—not even The Ten. It was always meant to destroy every bit of self-confidence we had so the only response left would be confidence in God. That's what eventually happened to me. I reached the end of myself because I realized that no matter how hard I tried I could never live up to the impossible standard. It was a devastating realization and it felt like my life had come to an end, but that put me in a prime position to receive life from Him.

Unfortunately, sin seized the opportunity of the Law to make us think we could actually carry it out, thereby adding fuel to the fire of the already raging pride of fallen man. It took a Law that was given to lead us to life in God (by destroying our reliance on self and making us see our need for reliance on Him) and it used it to convince us that Life could really be attained by our own efforts. In that, we see how sinful sin really is.

We may not come outright and admit it. In fact, many will agree with the paragraph above, but their actions will say different. They will say, "Amen! We don't find righteousness in the Law!" but they are still stressing and striving to keep those rules as a means to keep God off their back and keep Him pleased. That's not putting faith in Christ, that's putting faith in you. Even though our lips may confess that there is no righteousness to be gained through the Law, our hearts do not agree because we still try to achieve rightness with Him through our own ability to obey those rules.[4]

The verse in 2 Cor. 3 is saying that, even today, when the Law of Moses is emphasized, there is a veil in place over people's eyes and they become blind to the glory of God. Their minds cannot comprehend Him. As much as people say, "Jesus + Nothing," those same people are offended at the idea of "Jesus – The Law." They dread the thought of a Jesus apart from Moses. Their mind is closed to the person of Christ as long as it's open to the Law of Moses.

Why does this happen? Because again, the Law puts all of the focus on you and your efforts, and it completely blinds you to Him and His. It's like a father who gets so busy with his work that he unknowingly ignores the rest of his family. The family may speak to him, he may say, "uh huh. Yeah yeah," but his mind and his heart are focused elsewhere. The man is so into his own work that he has become blind to his family. Then it's justified in his mind by saying, "I'm doing this work *for* my family!" In the same way, we justify our religious works and blindness to God by saying, "I'm doing these things *for* God!"[5]

> "But when someone changes and follows the Lord, that covering is taken away." (ERV)

Many say, "I follow Jesus!" but most of their time is spent following Moses and trying to abide by those Laws. They are so focused on their own work that they can't see His. Above it says that when someone changes from living that way (trying to abide by the Law and your own works) and follows the Lord (abiding in Him and His works), the covering is taken away. What does that mean exactly? It means to quit trying to get (or stay) right with God by what you do, and accept that you are *already* right with God by what He has done for you. If you're going to make any effort, make every effort to rest from your work.[6]

The Letter Kills

During the six years I was stuck in sin and trying to obey all the rules, I probably would have said "Amen!" to most of the stuff in this book. Christians cheer for the verses about being free from sin and no longer under the Law, but most are actually oblivious to what it means because they continue trying to "obey the Lord's commands."

I'm in no way trying to insult those who do that, nor am I trying to diminish the Lord's commands, I'm simply saying that His obedience did more for you than your obedience could ever do, and just because you "amen" a Bible verse about freedom doesn't mean you believe it (I'm speaking from a lot of experience!).

> *"He made us able to be servants of a new agreement from himself to his people. It is not an agreement of written Laws, but it is of the Spirit. The written Law brings death, but the Spirit gives life." – 2 Cor. 3:6 (ERV)*

Much like Paul said in Romans 7, here he is telling his readers that the Law brings death. Why? Not because the Law is bad, but because the Law arouses sin, whose wages are death. On the contrary, this new covenant agreement is not like the old. The old was based on written Laws that resulted in death, but the new is based on the Spirit who gives life. If life could be gained through keeping the Law, we really wouldn't have needed the Spirit at all.

The Substitute

Near the end of Galatians 3 (which I consider to be one of the most important chapters [if not books] in the entire Bible), Paul uses the illustration that the Law was like a guardian to the Jewish people until the Messiah arrived.

Do you remember substitute days in school? Sometimes it would be a great day of rest where we didn't have to do anything. We would sit at our desk, watch a movie and eat popcorn. It was a Sabbath day of rest. Other times it would be obnoxious because you'd expect to do nothing, but the substitute would just relay work and tests from the teacher. And did you ever have a day where the substitute and the real teacher were there at the same time? Those were awkward. Much of the class would just stare at the substitute like, "Why are you here?"

Much like a substitute teacher, the Law was given to keep the students (the Jewish people) on track until the real Teacher arrived. In that time, they would obey what the substitute said, and do the work the substitute assigned. But what happens when the real teacher returns? You're no longer in need of the substitute, and you're no longer under their command because the real teacher is there to give you your assignments Himself.

Is the substitute bad? Not at all! They serve their purpose. They teach and keep the class in order while the real teacher is away. But that's the only time they have purpose in the classroom, for as soon as the real teacher arrives they get to go home, relieved of their duty.

In the same way, since the Teacher (Jesus) has arrived, the substitute (the Law) is no longer needed. We are no longer under their guidance because we now have the guidance of our real Teacher.[7]

> "Now that the way of faith has come, we no longer need the Law to be our guardian." – Galatians 3:25 (ERV)

A Shadow of Things to Come

> "So don't let anyone condemn you for what you eat or drink, or for not celebrating certain holy days or new moon ceremonies or Sabbaths. For these rules are only shadows of the reality yet to come. And Christ himself is that reality." – Col. 2:16-17 (NLT)

I talked about this a little bit in my book, *It's All About Jesus*, but if you want a really good examination of this topic, I recommend going on Youtube and searching for "Greg Boyd, From shadow to the reality in Christ." He presents a really good perspective on how "the shadow of things to come" relates to "the reality found in

Christ," and it has completely changed the way I read the Old Testament.

For now, I will use the verse above to emphasize the substitute analogy: that the old rules were like a substitute teacher, keeping watch over the classroom until the real Teacher arrived. But now, since the real Teacher is here, the substitute is no longer needed. In the verse above, Paul is telling the Colossian church, "Don't let anyone judge you by the guidelines given by the substitute teacher. Those things don't apply to you anymore." This is important because, as I will be shamelessly repeating throughout this book, sin gets its power from the Law.

When you try to live in the shadow you will find yourself in darkness, but when you live in the Light (the reality that is found in Christ), everything becomes clear. It's logical, right? A shadow only exists because something is blocking out the light. If Paul says the old way of doing things (the law-based old covenant) is a shadow, then it means that something is blocking out the light and keeping people in darkness. But when the obstacle is removed, the light shines brightly and the shadow disappears. Likewise, on the cross, Christ removed the obstacle of sin that was causing us to live in the shadows and stumble in the darkness. In Him, the light shines brightly, we see clearly, and the shadow has disappeared. (We will talk about this in chapter 3.)

Can't We Have Both?

There are a lot of people who will say, "Yes, grace has come. Yes, Jesus is here. But we *still* need the Law to keep us in line!" Truthfully, there's no biblical basis for such thinking. The verse people often pull out of scripture to say that the Law is still established is in Matthew 24.

> *"Heaven and earth will disappear, but my words will never disappear."*
> *Matthew 24:35 (NLT)*

There it is! Jesus said His words will never disappear. I'm not sure how that gets translated to "The Law will never disappear" though, because the context of the verse is Jesus talking about the coming destruction of the temple and the end of the old covenant ("the end of the age"). The destruction of the temple was a sign that the old religion has been done away with. It was never meant to inspire us to cheer for Israel to rebuild it, because that temple is a representation of the very thing that kept men separated from God.

The only reason Jesus is talking about the Law in the verse above is to say that the old, Law-based covenant is coming to end. It would make no sense for Jesus to tell his disciples, "The old way of doing things is coming to an end... but The Law (i.e. the old way of doing things) will never pass away!"

What?

It's true that the words of Jesus will never pass away, but scripture doesn't ever refer to "the Law" as "the words of Jesus." The Law is more often referred to as "The Law of Moses." Jesus, speaking to the Pharisees, even called it "your Law."[8]

The words of Jesus? They will never disappear. The Law of Moses? It already has! Jesus established a new covenant, and by doing so it means the old has been made obsolete and is ready to vanish.

> *"God called this a new agreement, so he has made the first agreement old. And anything that is old and useless is ready to disappear."* – Hebrews 8:13 (ERV)

Again in 2 Cor. 5:17,

> *"When anyone is in Christ, it is a whole new world. The old things are gone; suddenly, everything is new!" (ERV)*

Many people want the old and the new at the same time, but it makes no sense. If you upgrade to a 50-inch flat-screen TV, are you going to keep the old "bunny ears" around? No. It's obsolete. What good is it to you when you have this amazing new thing that's in every way better than the old thing? I no longer have to carry a 20-inch TV that weighs more than my car! The new one is lighter, bigger, and looks way better. The old TV may have served its purpose at one time, but to continue using it now would be a downgrade, while ignoring the new thing (the better thing) that has replaced it. Likewise, to run back to the Law would be a downgrade from what we've been given by God's grace through Christ.

Sewing Lessons from Heaven

Look at what Jesus said about trying to mix the old and the new (or have both at the same time).

> *"When someone sews a patch over a hole in an old coat, they never use a piece of cloth that is not yet shrunk. If they do, the patch will shrink and pull away from the coat. Then the hole will be worse. Also, no one ever pours new wine into old wineskins. The wine would break them, and the wine would be ruined along with the wineskins. You always put new wine into new wineskins." – Mark 2:21-22 (ERV)*

Jesus didn't come to patch the new together with the old and magically make them work together, but rather He came to make "all things new." Had He merely patched the new onto the old, the new would have torn away from the old and left a bigger hole than there was to begin with—the new cloth is not compatible with the old cloth.

Likewise, you don't pour new wine into old wineskins because old wineskins have already been stretched to their limits. They've taken all they can handle. If you try to save the old wineskin and reuse it with new wine, then the old wineskin will burst and ruin the new wine. The old cannot handle the new; new wine needs new wineskins.

What's the point?

Jesus didn't come to bring a new way of doing things that resembles the old way of doing things. Instead He came to bring a *better* way of doing things. And starting new is the only way it would last.

You might be a little frustrated with me over these things, or feel that I'm trying to attack God's Law, but I hope you will stick with me through the rest of this book and let things unfold. Many get mad at the things I've said so far because they're convinced that "God's Law is perfect!" But is it really? Let's look at scripture and see if that's actually true.

In chapter 4 through the rest of the book, we'll look at the sinful nature and the implications of the new creation. But I feel it's necessary to spend one more chapter showing you how the Law affects people (or rather, how sin affects people through the Law), so we know what we're dealing with when we try to live a life based on those old standards.

Endnotes

[1] See Matt. 5:27

[2] See Matt. 5:21

[3] See Mark 10:17-27

[4] Don't get defensive and put up walls if this applies to you. It applied to me as well. But the fix only came when I quit trying to hide behind my obsessive religious need to have it all together, and came right out and admitted that everything in my life had fallen apart. You don't have to admit it to me or anyone else; admitting it to yourself and your Father is enough. You're completely safe with Him and He won't use your confessions or vulnerabilities against you. Be bold with Him; completely out in the open, naked and exposed! Don't hide in fig leaves.

[5] If you want to see an incredibly good analogy of this, watch the movie *Click*, starring Adam Sandler

[6] See Heb. 4:10-11

[7] I know some will argue that the Law was given for Jewish people not Gentiles, so I shouldn't be talking as if it's for Christians at all. But this book is written to Gentiles who are convinced, like we once were, that the Law is for all. Therefore, that is the language I am choosing to use, rather than getting into semantics.

[8] See John 10:34

The Imperfect vs. The Perfect

As we've already discussed, it was the old rule-keeping way of life that empowered sin, which resulted in death. Christ didn't come to condemn us to that same perpetual roundabout in the new covenant, instead He came to unravel that endless circle and give us a way out of it.

Before we get into this chapter let me say that I know some of you might be thinking, "This is all great. But what does it have to do with living free from sin?" My logic for putting these chapters first is that in order to begin living free from sin, you first have to understand what is causing the cycle of sin in the first place. Am I telling you through all of this that the Law is bad? Or that's it's the thing causing us to sin? Or that you should rip the Old Testament out your Bibles? No. However, sin uses the Law to replicate itself. The Law, great as it was for its purpose at the time, isn't perfect (even though people will stubbornly insist that it is).

> *"If the first covenant had been faultless, there would have been no need for a second covenant to replace it." – Heb. 8:7 (NLT)*

If the old worked, we wouldn't have needed the new. But as it is, since the old was based on our ability rather than on God's, it came with many problems.

> *"The old rule is now ended because it was weak and worthless. The Law of Moses could not make anything perfect. But now a better hope has been given to us. And with that hope we can come near to God." – Hebrews 7:18-19 (ERV)*

We love to talk about how Jesus tore the veil and how we can now come near to God. That veil was a representation of an old covenant that kept God's glory hidden from the minds of men—it blinded them to the Lord. As Paul said, that veil is only taken away (torn down) in Christ. However, even though many quote those verses and sing songs about the veil being torn, they still try to live by that old set of rules that put the veil there in the first place.

The new agreement is based on better promises that bring life. In the new, the mystery of God is revealed to the world and nothing is kept hidden. So why do we continue trying to mix in an old agreement that's based on inferior promises that bring death and hide Life from us?

The Consequences of Preaching the Law

When we preach the Law, we are harming our congregations more than we realize. It all sounds fine on the surface: with good intentions, we're trying to keep people on track and obeying God's Laws so they can keep God happy. But there are still consequences of living under that old system. Here are 3 things scripture says happens when the Law is emphasized over the Lord.

1. We are giving sin more power over people's lives

"The sting of death is sin, and the power of sin is the Law." – 1 Cor. 15:56 (NIV)

Sin gets its power from the Law. I know we like to think that the more we preach the Law, the more we are empowering people to *quit* with their sinful behavior, but scripture clearly says that the opposite is true. When the Law is emphasized, sin gets more out of control than it would have otherwise been! Meaning, the more heavily we preach the Law, the more we are empowering sin to run rampant in our own lives, and the lives of others.

It seems backwards, I know. Logically it seems like more rules results in better behavior, but God seems to know something we don't about people's behavior. His way says that better behavior comes through showing grace and patience to those who behave badly, not by upping the amount of rules and threats of judgment for breaking them.

The quickest way to drain the life from sin is to quit living by the thing that gives it life in the first place. Do you remember what Paul said in Romans 7:8-9? Apart from the Law, sin is dead, and you are alive. But when the Law comes, you exchange places: sin comes alive, and you die.

I know this can be hard to hear because we seem to have thousands of years of traditions that say, "The way to defeat sin and please God is to obey the Ten Commandments!" but scripture, as I hope I've shown you, says the exact opposite over and over again!

2. We are putting people under a curse

In Galatians 3, the chapter that probably shows more clearly than any other that we aren't under Law, Paul makes the point (in verse 10) that those under the Law are under a curse.

> "But those who depend on the Law to make them right with God are under his curse, for the Scriptures say, "Cursed is everyone who does not observe and obey all the commands that are written in God's Book of the Law." (NLT)

A lot of people today think that if you just obey "The Ten," you'll be okay. They don't realize that there are over 600 Mosaic Laws in the old covenant, and if you break just one, you're guilty of breaking every single one! Even if you kept The Ten (1.6% of the entire Law), you still have over 600 more (98.4%) to go, otherwise all the effort given to The Ten was for nothing! Do you see how hopeless it is? You were never meant to carry that kind of burden. Trying to do so is indeed a continuous curse of disappointment and failure, and a constant awareness of both.

> "Is it not obvious to you that persons who put their trust in Christ (not persons who put their trust in the Law!) are like Abraham: children of faith? It was all laid out beforehand in Scripture that God would set things right with non-Jews by faith. Scripture anticipated this in the promise to Abraham: "All nations will be blessed in you."
>
> So those now who live by faith are blessed along with Abraham, who lived by faith—this is no new doctrine! And that means that anyone who tries to live by his own effort, independent of God, is doomed to failure. Scripture backs this up: "Utterly cursed is every person who fails to carry out every detail written in the Book of the Law."
>
> The obvious impossibility of carrying out such a moral program should make it plain that no one can sustain a relationship with God that way. The person who lives in right relationship with God does it by embracing what God arranges for him. Doing things for God is the opposite of entering into what God does for you." – Galatians 3:7-12 (MESSAGE)

3. We are leading people away from faith in Christ

We are saved by grace through faith, not by works. On the contrary, the Law is not based on faith.[1] The Law is based on reliance in yourself, not Jesus. In trying to live by the Law you are saying, "I can do it better than Him!" (Even if it's unintentional). Romans 7 is the result of that kind of thinking. It's a constant struggle to do good, and an endless experience of one failure after the other.

In Christ, the old covenant is made void and done away with. The veil is removed, not only from the temple, letting us boldly walk into the Holy of Holies (and even establishing it in our own bodies), but it's also removed from our eyes. No longer are we self-focused, now we are Christ-focused, set free from that guilt and self-condemnation that has plagued humanity since the Garden.

> "But whenever a person turns [in repentance] to the Lord, the veil is stripped off and taken away." – 2 Cor. 3:16 (AMP)

That's not a call to repent for your sin, but to repent of your obsession with the Law. It isn't sin that blinds you to the Lord, it's the self-righteousness that naturally follows the obsession with rule keeping. A lot of people repent enough to accept God's forgiveness, but not enough to have the veil removed so they can see what Christ has really accomplished for them, and accept the complete freedom from sin that's available.

Still Not Convinced?

If that's not enough to convince you, here's a more extensive list of verses that tell us the negative effects of the Law:
- The Law kills. (2 Cor. 3:6)
- The Law causes sin to increase. (Romans 5:20)

- The Law causes people to sin and die. (Romans 7:8-9).
- The Law is weak and worthless, an inferior hope that has been ended, and could never make anything perfect. (Heb. 7:18-19)
- The Law is full of faults (Heb. 8:7)
- The Law nullifies the work of Jesus (Gal. 2:21)
- The Law is not based on faith. (Galatians 3:12)
- The Law separates people from Christ and cuts them off from grace. (Gal. 5:4)
- The Law is only a shadow, not the reality found in Jesus. (Col. 2:17)
- The Law has been made obsolete. (Heb. 8:13)
- The Law is no longer needed. (Galatians 3:25)
- We are no longer under the Law. (Romans 6:11)

Through all of that, it's important to remember that "the law is holy, righteous and good" (Romans 7:12). I used to speak of the Law with disgust, as if it were just the most horrible thing in existence. Though all of the above is in scripture, it also says that the Law is not the whole problem. The overall problem with the Law is that sin uses vulnerabilities in the Law to reproduce more sin.

The Old Code is Vulnerable

Earlier this year I ran into a minor problem on my website. *It got hacked!* There was no sensitive information stolen, but the hacker added a bunch of hidden advertisements for Viagra and other "grown-up" medications. Although *most* people couldn't see the ads, there were a few times where somebody would post a link to my page on one of their news websites, and the link description on their site would show nothing but "Buy Viagra!" text. It was embarrassing to say the least, considering I had just released my first book and I was getting more traffic to my website than usual (what a first impression for new readers!).

How did the hacker find a way into my site? Well, in my busy little life as an aspiring author, I forgot to update the code used on my blog (the code is all the hidden information you don't see, that tells the website how it should appear and behave). I was at least two versions behind in updates, and hackers, as it turns out, spend all of their time looking for vulnerabilities in old code that they can use to sneak in through the backdoor of someone's site.

Sin, coincidentally enough, does the same thing with the Law. Although the Law itself is good, since it's an outdated code it holds many vulnerabilities and open doors for sin (like the virus it is) to sneak in and use a person's good intentions against them. That's what we see in Romans 7. Paul, speaking as a man under the Law (the old code), has all the good intentions in the world to obey the Law and do the right thing, but somehow sin is right there— "hacking" his actions in a sense—causing him to do the things he doesn't want to do.

What was the fix for my site? First I had to update everything to its most current version (and I've made sure to stay on top of it ever since!), and secondly my friend Rebecca had to go in and remove the problem code that was placed there by the hacker. Funny thing is, she had removed the problem code before, but because I didn't update my site right away, the problem came right back (such is the way of sin!). Had I not updated the code on my site, I would have had to keep calling her back every few days to fix the problem, and it would have kept returning. That would have gone on and on in a perpetual cycle, but because everything is up-to-date, the problem has since been resolved once for all!

This is what Jesus accomplished on the cross. In Hebrews 10, the writer says that in the old covenant they offered sacrifices for their sin year after year (a temporary fix), but those sacrifices could never perfect them or remove their guilt (if it could, they would have quit offering them). For them it was an ongoing thing. Since the overall code hadn't yet been updated, they had to keep going back and removing Viagra ads from their websites. But those ads would inevitably return because they had no way to update the vulnerable code—the backdoor was left wide open for sabotage.

Jesus, like my dear friend Rebecca, came and fixed the problem altogether. He not only offered one sacrifice to get the dirty code out of the system for good, He then updated the code of the system itself, ensuring that the problem could never return. He shut and sealed the backdoor, leaving sin with no way to get back in.

The problem is that a lot of Christians don't know the code has been updated and that the hacker's code (the sin nature that snuck into our bodies through the fall) has been removed. As a result, they continue living as if sin still exists in their bodies, though in actuality, it's long gone.

I think we've built a good enough foundation here. It's time to dive into the subject of the sinful nature and find out what exactly happened to yours (and mine)!

Endnotes

[1] See Eph. 2:8-10, Gal. 3:13

Death and Resurrection

A popular idea in the church today (one that many Christians share), is that it's our nature to sin and we will always sin until we die. It's an idea that says we have dual natures (the Spirit and the flesh) warring against each other, and our body is the battlefield these wars are waged on. We can't really do anything about it except cheer for the good guy and hope he wins out. Yet, as much as Jesus said, "The Spirit is willing, but the flesh is weak," under the belief of dual natures it more often sounds like the opposite is true: the flesh more often seems to win out over the Spirit. Somehow the pull of the devil always seems to be stronger than Jesus. We hear it in our church services all the time, as we are told over and over how wicked we are, and how much we need to stop being so displeasing to God, and these things influence the way we communicate with Him.

Crucified

Now, we in the church talk a whole lot about the crucifixion of Jesus. It's understandable since that's the *entire foundation* of our faith. However, what often fails to get mentioned (or at least elaborated on) is how much we were on that cross with Him.

"Crucified with Christ" is often another one of those things we casually quote, but don't really understand the full implications of. Look at the following verse.

> *"Those who belong to Christ Jesus have nailed the passions and desires of their sinful nature to his cross and crucified them there." – Galatians 5:24 (NLT)*

We don't have to get into the graphic details of how a crucifixion works, just know that it inevitably kills whoever is put up there. The verse above is confirming what we briefly talked about in Chapter 1—that we died with Christ. We obviously haven't experienced a *physical* death or crucifixion (thankfully He did that part!), but we did experience the spiritual death of our sinful selves (that part of us that was ruled and controlled by pride and selfish desires). In the verse above, Paul makes it very clear that the sinful nature was crucified on the cross with Christ—it died. And yet, somehow, many of us still fell for the idea that it's still alive in us, creeping around and luring us into sin. We confess in prayer how "sinful" and "wretched" we are, calling ourselves "unworthy servants" and thinking these things impress God. But neither Jesus nor Paul ever called us such things.

A lot of people will nod and say, "Yes, yes. I know this already! We're dead to sin!" but many of those same people will go to church and give just as confident of a nod to the pastor when he says we still have a sinful nature and a wicked heart, or we are still "fallen" and prone to sin. I don't want you to just nod at the things in this book. Think about what they really mean. Let it sink in.

If your sinful nature (that is, the entire person that was corrupted and controlled by sin) was crucified with Christ, then that person died along with Christ. How can you say, "I was crucified with Christ," and then turn around and say, "I still have a sinful nature" when it was that sinful nature that was crucified with Christ? That's what that verse above is about. The sinful nature was done away with. It's not hanging on by the tips of its fingers, or trying to keep one foot in your life. It was killed, dragged outside the city, and buried.

This is great news!

Wanted: Dead AND Alive

"So I am not the one living now—it is Christ living in me. I still live in my body, but I live by faith in the Son of God. He is the one who loved me and gave himself to save me." – Galatians 2:20 (ERV)

The above is probably one of the most popular verses in scripture. Yet, even the people who quote it most often follow it up by saying things in prayer like, "I'm so unworthy! I'm so sinful. My heart is wicked! I can't do the good I want to do! Fix me, Jesus!"

Please don't take that as if I'm picking on you—I've prayed all of those prayers, and many more. But I eventually had to ask myself, "If I truly believe that I no longer live, why am I talking as if I'm still alive? If that old person was crucified with Christ, why do I speak like they've somehow survived? If Christ lives in me, why do I talk so bad about myself all the time?"

That old person and everything that was corrupt about him is gone. You'll never see that person again—they have ceased to exist. That means I don't approach God as that person anymore, crying to

Him, "Look at me! Look at how alive sin is in my body!" because no matter how much I try to convince Him of it, He won't see what isn't there.

I apologize if it feels like I'm repeating myself or scolding you, but some of this stuff bears repeating so it sinks in and isn't just casually looked over and forgotten. I want you to see how wishy-washy this gets when people don't truly understand what happened to them at the cross. That's not in any way to pretend that I've never looked over this stuff or prayed the kinds of prayers I mentioned above. I have (a lot!). But that was only until I found out that those prayers were already answered for me 2,000 years ago.

Throughout my whole misery trip of having severe anger problems and manipulating girls, I would often quote the verses that say, "I no longer live, Christ lives in me!" But I could never understand the implications of those things because the veil of the Law (the demand for my personal performance) was so heavy over my eyes. I was a workaholic. With that veil over my eyes all I could see was, "I need to do more! I need to work harder! I need to be stronger! I need to keep trying! I just need more faith!" I was putting all of my effort into getting something out of my body that He already got out of my body through His effort (even though I quoted all the verses about how my faith was in Him, and we aren't saved by works).

Many Christians forget to do what Paul said to do in Romans 6: "Consider [think of] yourselves as dead to sin, but alive to God in Christ." If I'm truly going to think of myself as dead to sin, that means I get to stop talking as if it's still alive in my body. I get to approach God and say, "Thank you that I'm not wicked or unworthy or sinful! Thank you that I'm forever dead to those things that sabotaged my thoughts and emotions and relationships! Thank you that I'm alive to you and your goodness forever! Thank you that I have been created in Christ to do *good* works!"

So am I only dead to sin every time I bow a knee at the repentance altar? Am I only dead to sin whenever I confess my sins and ask God to forgive me? Am I only dead to sin when I have a good day and don't feel any temptations to do something I know I shouldn't? Too what extent do I consider myself dead to sin?

> *Yes, when Christ died, he died to defeat the power of sin one time—enough for all time. He now has a new life, and his new life is with God. **In the same way**, you should see yourselves as being dead to the power of sin and alive for God through Christ Jesus. – Romans 6:10-11 (ERV)*

In what same way? "One time—enough for all time." That is the death you and I have died to sin because that's the death He died to sin. It's not a temporary death until the next time we sin, and then that nature resurrects itself and drags us away in chains. That thing died one time—enough for all time ("Once for all" in most translations). Now, just as Christ has risen to new life, and His new life is with God, *in the same way,* you have risen to new life with God as well. That is how you are told to think of yourself. Not as an unworthy wretch who is forever trapped in a circle of sin.

Don't Complicate It

It doesn't matter how much you quote the Bible, it's about how much you really believe what it says. It's not as complicated as some of the expert scholars and professors like to make it with unnecessary paradoxes. The kingdom of God isn't complicated. Although the accomplishments of the cross are vast, they aren't meant to be confusing.

You died with Him and you were raised to new life with Him. The death He died to sin once for all you also died to sin once for all.

The life He now lives to God you also live to God. You are hidden in Him and have been made like Him. Where He goes, you go. Where you go, He goes. You are one Spirit with the Lord.

That's only a small part of what the cross did, but it it's only meant to be complicated for those who are self-proclaimed to be wise. And the only reason it's complicated to them is because they can't comprehend how something so wonderful could be so simple. Many will add unnecessary complexities to this message to make it sound like they have more wisdom and understanding about these things. Meanwhile, it was unschooled men who carried this message around the world, and the when the Pharisees heard them speak, what was their conclusion? "They have been with Jesus." They didn't have degrees in complex theology, but they knew the Gospel because they knew the Person. [1]

The cross wasn't strictly for the forgiveness of sins, but to remove sin from you *entirely*. He didn't "cover" your sin, as if to sweep it under the carpet of blindness and denial, He "took away" your sin as if to cast it forever into the deepest sea. [2]

> *"And I will forgive the wrongs they have done, and I will not remember their sins." – Heb. 8:12 (ERV)*

He forgot about your sin, now it's your turn to do the same!

Snip, Snip!

> *"When you came to Christ, you were 'circumcised,' but not by a physical procedure. Christ performed a spiritual circumcision—the cutting away of your sinful nature." – Col. 2:11 (NLT)*

Under the Law, there is this thing that every Jewish male must endure, called circumcision. I'm sure most of you know what it is, but for the sake of the analogy, I'll still have to explain it. (Good thing we're all grown-ups here!)

Circumcision is defined as "the cutting off of the foreskin of males that is practiced as a religious rite by Jews and Muslims and as a sanitary measure in modern surgery."

The foreskin, if you're not aware, is an extra piece of flesh that grows on the male penis (go ahead and get the giggles out of your system; I said "penis" in a Christian book!). The foreskin isn't a necessary part of the body, which is often why it's removed—it serves no purpose. Not to be gross or give you too much information about myself, but I was circumcised when I was a baby. Do you know what's exciting about that? The foreskin that was removed from my body hasn't been chasing me around for 27 years, trying to reattach itself. That would be scary (and it would make an interesting, yet very awkward horror film).

Joking aside, when that piece of skin was "cut off," it did what anything else does when it's removed from its life source: it shriveled up and died! (For a less adult illustration, think of pulling a leaf or a piece of fruit off of a tree. It dies soon after.)

Under the effects of the fall, man became the life source of the sinful nature. That nature was like a leech and our flesh is what gave it sustenance. The terrible part is that we couldn't remove it; it became a part of us. So, just as the Bible is filled with many other types and shadows (metaphors of things that were to happen in the future), the Jewish people began circumcising themselves, starting with Abraham (who was like 1000 years old at the time, so it probably hurt a lot). But this was done as a representation of what the Messiah would come and do when He arrived. He would perform a spiritual circumcision, removing that unnecessary part of the flesh from our bodies forever. How do we know it's forever?

Because remember, when that piece of flesh is removed from its life source, it shrivels up and dies.

Working in Tandem

So then, just as the action of sin found its nourishment in the Law, the condition of sin found its nourishment in the flesh. Sin took advantage of the Law because it aroused the sinful desires of the flesh (that is, the sinful nature). This is why we found ourselves in a perpetual cycle of uncontrollable sin. We really couldn't do anything about it because sin was connected to us—it was a part of our body. However, what's the gospel ("good news")? That Christ made the Law obsolete, and removed the sinful nature from our body. He took away the two things that were giving sin its strength in our lives (the Law and the sin nature).

He disarmed and defeated sin in one fell swoop!

> "You were dead because of your sins and because your sinful nature was not yet cut away. Then God made you alive with Christ, for he forgave all our sins. He canceled the record of the charges against us and took it away by nailing it to the cross. In this way, he disarmed the spiritual rulers and authorities. He shamed them publicly by his victory over them on the cross." – Col. 2:13-15 (NLT)

Or my favorite translation,

> "He stripped all the spiritual tyrants in the universe of their sham authority at the Cross and marched them naked through the streets." – (MESSAGE)

As you can see, He spared no expenses and He cut no corners. When He came to deal with the sin issue, it wasn't to cover it up or sweep it under the carpet until the Second Coming. He dealt with the issue directly and thoroughly. In doing so He set us completely free from the problem altogether, rather than a partial freedom that will only be completed through physical death. Jesus was all about changing our reality in this life, not delaying change until some unknown date in the future. He didn't come to deliver the message that said, "One day you'll be free," but rather to say, "I have come to set you free today." His message wasn't that the Kingdom of God was coming, but that it was here. "The Kingdom of God is at hand!" And Paul followed suit when he said, "*Now* is the time of salvation."[3]

Don't push into the future what Christ has provided in the present.

Endnotes

[1] No. This doesn't mean I'm against religious education or Bible college. I'm only making the point that it's not a requirement in order to truly grasp this gospel message. You only need to get to know the Person and what He has done for you.

[2] See John 1:29, Micah 7:19

[3] 2 Cor. 6:2. The word salvation there is the Greek word "sōtēria" (Strong's G4991). It doesn't only mean going to heaven when you die. It covers deliverance from sin, sickness, death, judgment, wrath, and a whole lot more. The exact wording the concordance uses is "deliverance from the molestation of enemies."

The Myth of Dual Natures

It's a very popular idea today that Christians have dual natures. This idea says that, although the Spirit of Jesus lives in us, darkness lives in us as well. In other words, although our body is the temple of the Holy Spirit, the devil is His housemate. This is one of the many damaging doctrines that have come from a sin-focused interpretation of Romans 7. Since we already talked about Romans 7, we won't do much of that here, but I'll quickly point out the verses that often get used to back up this idea that Christians have two natures.

> "As it is, it is no longer I myself who do it, but it is sin living in me. For I know that good itself does not dwell in me, that is, in my sinful nature. For I have the desire to do what is good, but I cannot carry it out. For I do not do the good I want to do, but the evil I do not want to do—this I keep on doing. Now if I do what I do not want to do, it is no longer I who do it, but it is sin living in me that does it.
>
> So I find this law at work: Although I want to do good, evil is right there with me. For in my inner being I delight in God's law; but I see another law at work in me, waging war against the law of my mind and making me a prisoner of the law of sin at work within me." – Romans 7:17-23 (NIV)

As we already talked about in Chapter 1, Paul was speaking as a man under the law who was still enslaved to sin, not as a man under grace who has been set free. This Romans 7 man has yet to share in the benefits of Christ's work. He is hopelessly tugged around by the sin in his body, and forced to do things he doesn't want to do. He's in a constant state of condemnation and disappointment. For this man, sin does live in his body and it's waging war against his mind, which demands that he do what he cannot do, "Obey God's Law!"

This is not a man who is under the grace of Jesus, but under the heavy burden of the Law, apart from Christ. He's not a man who is partially in the light and partially in the darkness (as the dual nature belief goes), but a man who is hopelessly and fully trapped in darkness.

Out of Darkness, Into Light

"But you are his chosen people, the King's priests. You are a holy nation, people who belong to God. He chose you to tell about the wonderful things he has done. He brought you out of the darkness of sin into his wonderful light."
– 1 Peter 2:9 (ERV)

The verse above says that you were brought *out* of one thing (darkness) and *into* another (light). It doesn't say that you were left in limbo somewhere in the middle, straddling the fence between darkness and light, hoping you fall into the light but trying desperately not to fall into the darkness. Instead, it's actually good news: you were removed from darkness, and placed into the light.

You're no longer walking in the darkness of sin, nor do you need to walk in that darkness ever again. Just as the Israelites were taken out of slavery in Egypt and brought into the Promised Land, you were taken out of darkness and brought into the light. When the Israelites got to the Promised Land, were they simultaneously in

Egypt? No. They could only be in one place or the other, and thank God He had taken them to a better place and not left them stranded somewhere in between.

"But wait, what about the desert?"

Indeed! There are many desert songs nowadays that speak as if we're like those Israelites, stuck in between Egypt and the Promised Land, but the truth is we have reached our destination, which is relationship with Jesus. We're not in the desert, desperately struggling through the sand trying to reach this mysterious location—Jesus is the location, and He lives in us (and us in Him).

The only reason they were stuck in a desert was because of their disobedience and failure to take hold of what God had already provided for them. They grumbled and complained about what they *didn't* have and completely ignored everything God had already given them. (This still happens today, which leads many to relate to those people trapped in the desert, thinking God is the one who has put them there. But as we will get into more in the next chapter, the problem is a perception in the mind; it's a lack of awareness and acknowledgment of what God has already provided. ["My people perish for lack of knowledge."])[1]

This Little Light of Mine...

"In the past you were full of darkness, but now you are full of light in the Lord. So live like children who belong to the light." – Eph. 5:8 (ERV)

Just as Peter made a contrast between "out" and "in," once again we see a contrast between two things, past and present. In the past you were full of darkness, but now ("in the present") you are full of light. It's important to see that you don't just have a little light to let shine, but you're *full* of light. Since you are *full* of light, there's no room for darkness.

I really like the implications of some other translations.

> *"For you were once darkness, but now you are light in the Lord. Live as children of light..." (NIV)*

This one is my favorite because it says you *are* light. Light is not just something you have, it's someone you are. So how hard is it to live as children of light when you are full of light, and it's who you are in the Lord? Logically speaking, it should be a natural occurring thing, not a terrible struggle, right?

When you really begin to understand that this light isn't like some fragile spiritual lantern that you recklessly carry around, but it's something that has been merged with your very being (because "you are one spirit with the Lord"), and that you are not only full of light, but you are light, it changes the way you carry yourself. No longer do you walk around downtrodden, expecting to wake up to another day of being dragged off into darkness against your will and violated by the devil, instead you realize that you actually have the advantage, and that little snake is terrified of you. Knowing these things also changes the way you respond to darkness. You no longer feel the need to run from "sinners," afraid that their darkness is going to get on you or contaminate your holiness. Instead you love to be around people in darkness because you know that you're full of light, and the only possible outcome is that your light will displace the darkness around them. There's a good reason Jesus chose to hang out in dingy houses with prostitutes, drunks and thieves. He could do so without fear that they were going to influence His behavior or dim His light, because He knew who He was and what lived inside Him. He didn't see their darkness as a threat to His light, He saw His light as a threat to their darkness, and His light would set them free from that darkness. Not by force and coercion, but as a natural result of who He is.

Many will quote verses about having light, but they're terrified that any little flicker of sin will burn the bulb out. Therefore they do exactly what Jesus said not to do and hide their light in church buildings, never letting it benefit anyone unless the people on the outside come through the doors and behold their glorious collection of candles.

Many act as if this light is powered by their good behavior and ability to obey God, so if they don't act right or if they hang around the wrong person, then the light will be snuffed out and the bulb of righteous glory will once again need be changed at the next altar call. I used to believe that way as well, and I spent a lot of time trying to change spiritual light bulbs at church altars. It would make sense if the light was dependent on my power, but the good news is, it isn't! We are the conduits of light, not the generators. He's the power source; we're the ones who His power flows through.

Jesus is the Light of the World

When Jesus spoke again to the people, he said, "I am the light of the world. Whoever follows me will never walk in darkness, but will have the light of life." – John 8:12 (NIV)

If you read my first book, *It's All About Jesus*, you might remember when I talked about John 6, where Jesus says whoever follows Him will never hunger or thirst again. I was talking about it in the context of people in the desert, who were constantly looking for God to give them something new, while ignoring everything He had already given them. I compared it to how people today often talk about how they are hungry and thirsty for the Lord, despite the fact that He clearly said that anyone who receives Him will **never** hunger or thirst again (because they will be made full).

In the same way, in the verse above Jesus says that whoever follows Him will **never** walk in darkness, but will have the light of life. This is an easy one to glance over since we hear it so much, but when you look at the definition of the word "never," it's really exciting!

Never[2] (adverb) —

1. not ever : at no time

2. not in any degree : not under any condition.

Now let's look at the verse again.

> When Jesus spoke again to the people, he said, "I am the light of the world. Whoever follows me will never [not ever; at no time; not in any degree; not under any condition] walk in darkness, but will have the light of life." – John 8:12

The idea of dual natures completely ignores what Jesus said here. It insists that not only will we continue walking in darkness until we die, but darkness itself actually lives in us (and will continue to until it's purged from us through a physical death). If this is true, then what did Jesus actually even change?

"Well, He came to forgive our sins!"

Awesome! I'm so thankful for that. But what good is it for me to save you from being hit by a speeding car if you're prone to walking into traffic? Wouldn't it be better to help you fix whatever it is that causes you to jump in front of traffic in the first place? Otherwise it doesn't matter how much I push you out of the way of speeding vehicles, you're always going to get right back up and walk right back in front of them. That's not "good news" for you, because it's only a matter of time before you get flattened.

As we already examined in the last chapter, Jesus *did* forgive our sins, but He also took away the thing that was causing us to sin in the first place. He didn't only push us out of the way of traffic, He also empowered us to stay out of it by removing the thing that drew us into it.

Lifeguard on Duty

This would be the cue for some to say, "If we could live without sin, then we wouldn't need Jesus!" So then I propose this question: is a lifeguard on duty as proof that you're going to drown, or are they there just in case you do?

> *"My dear children, I write this to you so that you will not sin. But if anybody does sin, we have an advocate with the Father—Jesus Christ, the Righteous One." – John 2:1 (NIV)*

If anybody drowns, we have a lifeguard. But I write this to you so that you will not drowned. What's the point? It's possible to live your life without drowning. But on the off chance that you do drowned, there is a lifeguard on duty to help you out. So then, I'm not living my life trying not to drowned, I'm just enjoying the opportunity to learn how to swim; and should I make a mistake and get pulled out into the ocean, there's a lifeguard looking out for me.

You Are the Light of the World

> *"You are the light of the world. A town built on a hill cannot be hidden." – Matt. 5:14 (NIV)*

Jesus said before that He is the light of the world, but here He says you are the light of the world. Surely He couldn't be serious! You're full of sin and darkness, evil desires and temptations! Somehow He didn't seem to put that disclaimer in His statement.

How is it that you're the light of the world? Because you are following Jesus, which means you have the light of life in you. Remember what He said in the verse above? "Whoever follows me will never walk in darkness, but will have the light of life." Do you follow Jesus? Then you have the light of life, and you will never walk in darkness. You may sometimes *think* or *feel* like you're walking in darkness, but those thoughts and feelings aren't the truth. How do I know? Because Jesus said you will **never** *[not ever; at no time; not in any degree; not under any condition]* walk in darkness.

Again, in John 12:46, He says,

> "I have come into the world as a light, so that no one who believes in me should stay in darkness." (NIV)

Why did He come into the world? So you would spend the rest of your life in a desperate struggle, with one foot in darkness and the other in light? No. He came into the world so that no one who believes in Him should stay in darkness.

> "For God, who said, 'Let light shine out of darkness,' made his light shine in our hearts to give us the light of the knowledge of God's glory displayed in the face of Christ." - 2 Corinthians 4:6 (NIV)

You're not half full of light, and half full of darkness; you're completely full of light. The glass isn't half-empty and half-full, but it's completely filled to the brim and overflowing with the living water of Jesus. Then why is it that so many people are unable to live like that's true? Because it doesn't matter whether you're standing in a room full of light if you have a veil pulled over your face. Go on and try it! Turn on every light in your house and then pull your shirt over your face and try to walk around. You'll still stumble about as if you're walking through the darkness, even though you're standing in the light. (We'll talk about this more in the next chapter).

> *"You are all children of the light and children of the day. We do not belong to the night or to the darkness."- 1 Thessalonians 5:5 (NIV)*

Again, you're not in the darkness, you're fully in the light.

> *"This is the message we have heard from him and declare to you: God is light; in him there is no darkness at all." – 1 John 1:5 (NIV)*

Col. 3:3 says your life is hidden with Christ. Where is it hidden? In God. Is there any darkness in God? No. "In Him there is no darkness at all." Where are you? In Him! What's the conclusion? There is no darkness in you! If there was darkness in you, and you are in Him, that would mean there is darkness in Him.

> *"**In the past** you were full of darkness, **but now** you are full of light in the Lord. So live like children who belong to the light." – Eph. 5:8 (ERV)*

Dead and Gone

Do you remember what we talked about in the last chapter? The old sinful nature has been crucified with Christ. It has been completely removed from you just as a foreskin is removed during circumcision. That unneeded piece of flesh isn't hanging on by a thread, trying to make one last stand before you get to heaven. It has shriveled up and died. Now you are free to "consider yourselves dead to sin, but alive to God in Christ" without constantly living in a state of fear and paranoia, thinking the old dead man is looking for any opportune moment to jump out of the bushes and tackle you to the ground.

Contrary to popular belief, when you sin you're not acting according to your nature, you're acting outside of your nature because your nature is to act like Jesus, and Jesus never sinned. Darkness was the old nature, but it has been completely removed. You have been taken out of it, and brought into the light.

The reason this is difficult for some people to comprehend is because of how sin twisted our perception in the Garden when it turned our focus inward towards ourselves. We aren't able to see God's goodness as it truly is because we're so distracted by our "badness." Many Christian prayers, though heartfelt and genuine, are all about how wretched and filthy they are, and the goodness of God becomes a side-note at the end as a way to butter Him up while we ask Him to spare our wicked lives.

I grew up as a Christian who was terrified of thinking of myself as anything like Jesus. Even though we're told to try our hardest to be "Christ-like" we simultaneously believe it to be impossible to be like Christ. And when somebody dares to say, "I can be like Him!" all the same people who will tell you to be "Christ-like" are all of the sudden offended.

Back then, the very implication that I resembled Jesus in any way was offensive to me because I thought it offended God. Our perception of God is often that He's sitting in heaven with germaphobia, and any hint of human dirt just grosses Him out and ruins His entire day. We're not the only religion who feels that way about their God, most of them do. The only difference is that most of the other foreign gods really *are* offended by the sight of mere mortals. Ours was so unoffended that He actually *became* one of us and dwelt among us (and more often with the worst of us!).

In the next chapter I want look further into how the sin nature affected mankind—mainly how it corrupted our perception of God and ourselves—and then how Jesus restored what was lost.

Endnotes

[1] See Hebrews 4, Hos. 4:6
[2] Definition taken from Merriam-Webster.com

First Adam Separates Us

If you're a Christian, you've undoubtedly heard the story of Adam and Eve, and the fall of man. Since it's a popular story, we won't go into *too much* detail here. However, I do want to look at the fall of Adam and then (in the next chapter) the redemptive work of Jesus, who is referred to as the second (or last) Adam.

We'll start from the very beginning just to get some context and I'll include some of my personal perspectives of the Garden story (hoping they aren't too heretical for anybody to handle!).

In knowing what The Fall gave us we will better understand what the work of Jesus took away.

In The Beginning...

Fortunately, we've already dealt with Romans 7 and talked about how sin takes advantage of the Law and uses it to entice people to live a life of sin. Now we'll look at a practical example of that happening.

We know that God created Adam, placed him in the Garden and gave him *one* command,

> *"You may eat from any tree in the garden. But you must not eat from the tree that gives knowledge about good and evil. If you eat fruit from that tree, on that day you will certainly die!" – Gen. 2:16-17 (ERV)*

We see no sign yet that Adam was suddenly tempted to disobey the command. Next, God knocked Adam out (probably with a left jab), and while Adam was sleeping God took one of his ribs and used it to create Woman. Adam, full of excitement in verse 23 of Genesis 2, says, "Finally! Someone like me—bone from my bone, and flesh from my flesh!" It was love at first sight!

Now jump down to verse 25 (or just turn the page) and notice that the writer of Genesis thinks it's important to inform the reader that both of them were naked, yet neither of them felt shame. I think this is an important observation, because it will emphasize one of the most damaging things sin did to us.

Sin in Action

Now at this point, both man and woman are in the Garden. There's still no sign of them feeling tempted to eat from the Tree. But the serpent eventually shows up and tempts them, and they fall into sin. Let's look at how the serpent pulls this off.

> *The snake was the most clever of all the wild animals that the Lord God had made. The snake spoke to the woman and said, "Woman, did God really tell you that you must not eat from any tree in the garden?"*
>
> *The woman answered the snake, "No, we can eat fruit from the trees in the garden. (3) But there is one tree we must not eat from. God told us, 'You must not eat fruit from the tree that is in the middle of the garden. You must not even touch that tree, or you will die.'"*

But the snake said to the woman, "You will not die. (5) God knows that if you eat the fruit from that tree you will learn about good and evil, and then you will be like God!" – Genesis 3:1-5 (ERV)

Just as Paul said sin does with the commands of the Law, the serpent did with the command, "Do not eat from this tree." He took a good command that was meant for life, and he used it to bring death by enticing the woman to disobey. (Notice as well that this sinful desire is not originating in their heart, or coming from their nature. Temptation is not an automatic sign that they are wicked. If it were, then we can say Jesus was wicked since He too was tempted).

Have you ever believed something for really long, and then one day you say it aloud and all of the sudden the lights go on and you think, "Wow. That sounds really stupid now that I've said it." Perhaps (and this is pure assumption on my part) this is what Eve felt after the serpent got her to confess the command aloud. Because notice that he wiggles around it and doesn't actually repeat the command word-for-word himself? Instead he gets her to say it, and then uses *her* perspective of the command against her.

"Did God really say you must not eat from **any** tree in the garden?" He asks.

"Not **any** tree," Eve replies. "But only this special one in the middle."

"Oh?" says the serpent. "And you don't find it strange that you can eat from **any** tree except for this special one? Why do you suppose that is?"

"Because God said if we eat from that tree, we will die."

"Oh? Is that what He said? You won't *really* die. But God knows that if you eat from that tree you will learn about good and evil, and then you'll be like Him."

Eve looks at the tree again and considers what she's been told. "Yeah. Why would I die just from eating some fruit?" All of the sudden the tree starts to gain appeal. She never noticed it before, but this tree is actually really beautiful, and the fruit it bears looks delicious (plus, having the wisdom of God doesn't sound too bad!).

She goes for it. She reaches up, pulls down what was probably not an apple, and eats it. Then she notices Adam is right next to her, so she offers him a taste as well. "Here, eat this fruit, Husband, and then we will be like God!"

And like the faithful husband he was, Adam doesn't argue with his wife!

Sin-Consciousness

Suddenly their eyes open. They realize they are naked and immediately feel ashamed. They cover their eyes with one hand, their private parts with another, and run to the nearest fig tree to sew some makeshift clothes.

Then they hear a terrible sound being carried on the breeze of that cool day—*God's footsteps!* He's taking His daily stroll through the Garden and He's most definitely going to be *livid* when He finds out they disobeyed Him—more importantly, when He sees that *they're naked*. (*Ew!*)

They hid in the shadow of the trees, but God called out to Adam, "Where are you?"

Adam answered back from the darkness, "I'm here. I heard you in the Garden, but I was afraid because I'm naked; so I hid."

It was like the moment in a child's life when they become conscious of their body, and they make sure that nobody (not even their own mother and father) sees them naked, even though they had been seen naked a hundred times before! "Don't look!" they scream, while trying to keep their cheeks from turning red. All of the sudden it becomes embarrassing and shameful to be exposed, even though you've been exposed that way before and it never bothered you. That's what Adam experienced (although I'm sure it came with a lot more shame and guilt than a 6-year-old experiences when they grow past mom giving them a bath).

God asks the all-important question, "Who told you that you were naked? Have you eaten from that tree I commanded you not to eat from?"

Notice that God doesn't address their sin first? Instead He asks them how they knew to be ashamed of their nakedness. Who told them that being naked is wrong? They did.

Did God address them in an angry tone? That's what I grew up believing, but I don't think so anymore. He said it in the tone of a concerned father. "I told you not to do that. Now you're going to have to deal with the consequences I warned you about."

Adam says to the Lord, "It was the woman *you* put here with me—*she* gave me fruit from the tree, and I ate it!" Do you notice the immediate impulse towards self-preservation? This is only one of the many results of the fall. We look for the closest person we can blame for a problem we helped create so we can preserve our own safety and reputation, even if it's at the cost of theirs. Our first instinct in the fallen nature is to consider ourselves better than others. It's opposite of the nature of the Spirit, which is to "consider others better than yourselves."[1] In Adam's case, he's pretty much telling God, "If you're going to punish anyone over this, punish her! She did it!" So much for the whole "bone from my bone, flesh from my flesh" thing.

God looks at the woman and says, "What's the deal, Eve? I thought I was pretty clear about the ONE rule."

Self-preservation kicks in again. Her new flesh instinct is to look around for someone she can blame. She can't blame the lion, he can't talk yet; she can't blame the bear, he was sleeping (or stealing picnic baskets); *Ah ha!* "It was the serpent! He deceived me! If you're going to punish anyone over this, punish the serpent!"

Now, is there punishment in the Garden that day? *Absolutely!* In verses 14 – 19 we see God pronounce curses over the serpent, over the woman, and over the man. Personally, I'm unsure of how many of these curses were given by God, or how many of them were merely Him explaining the consequences they would have to endure as a result of their disobedience. For the serpent and the woman He seems to say, "I'm going to do these things..." but when He gets to Adam, He says, "Because of you, these things will happen..." I think one could argue both ways, although many people are more inclined to believe God anxiously handed out a whooping for their disobedience. For some strange reason we Christians love the idea that God punishes people harshly whenever they disobey... unless of course it's us doing the disobeying (wink, wink).

Let me tell you why I don't believe God punished them severely, blinded by righteous anger.

Punishment or Protection?

After God pronounces the curses and consequences caused by their sin, Adam *finally* names his wife (he was probably referring to her as "Hey, woman" before, which is probably the reason she ate from the tree in the first place. Women hate it when you refer to them that way!). But then we see that God starts preparing to send them packing.

Growing up, I always read their banishment from the Garden as if God was furious with them. As if He said, "Fine! You don't obey my rules? You don't deserve to live here anymore! *Get out!*" But the more I learned to line scripture up with the life of Jesus, and see the Father He perfectly displayed, the more my perspective of this story began to change. I welcome you to disagree, but regardless, the following is my current perspective.

> "The Lord God used animal skins and made some clothes for the man and his wife. Then he put the clothes on them." – Genesis 3:21 (ERV)

Here we see the first animal sacrifice in the Bible (in history for that matter). Why did God sacrifice this animal and put clothes on them? Because they were naked. And because of that nakedness they were ashamed. In the same way, what happens in our church services so often today is we spend all of our time shaming ourselves, thinking we're showing God how humble we are by telling Him that we're good for nothing dirt bags. "We're so unworthy, God!", "We're just sinners saved by grace!", or "We are worms, not men!" But from the very beginning, God showed how much He *didn't* want sin and shame to be our primary focus. He wasted no time covering the part that was causing them to focus on their shame. He didn't do it because He was ashamed of them, but because they had become ashamed of themselves.

> "The Lord God said, 'Look, the man has become like us—he knows about good and evil. And now the man might take the fruit from the tree of life. If the man eats that fruit, he will live forever.'" – Genesis 3:22 (ERV)

Again, I always read that verse as if God was saying, "Yeah. They went and disobeyed my command! Now they can't have this awesome thing I was going to give them. They don't deserve it anymore!" As if He's a bratty child who only wants to be your friend and share his toys with you when you do what He says, otherwise He cries and makes threats like "You're not my friend anymore!" I doubt anyone would come right out and say God sounds like that, but that's often how we make Him sound.

Think of this from God's point of view as He looks over this creature He created and realizes that man has become like Him, knowing good and evil. He sees that man has done evil, and as a consequence has become self-conscious and self-condemned. Man has the horrible feeling of shame and guilt that was never designed by God. So ask yourself, what happens if this man, who has become full of sin-consciousness and guilt (that causes an endless loop of more sin-consciousness and guilt), goes and eats from a tree that will cause him to live forever? It will literally be eternal condemnation for him and every person he fathers. Everyone from Adam on down will be stuck in a perpetual cycle of sin, guilt, shame and condemnation, and not even death itself could set them free because death couldn't touch them. It would be the eternal torment of hell without all of the the scary flames.

God wasn't throwing a temper tantrum when He banished them. He was doing what was in the best interest of His creation, which was to get them as far away from the Tree of Life as He could so He could actually bring a remedy to the curse without them making the curse permanent.

> "So the Lord God forced the man out of the Garden of Eden to work the ground he was made from. God forced the man to leave the garden. Then he put Cherub angels and a sword of fire at the entrance to the garden to protect it. The sword flashed around and around, guarding the way to the tree of life." – Genesis 3:23 (ERV)

He forced man out of the Garden and set up angels and a sword of fire to protect it from man. The sword flashed in front of the Tree of Life making sure nobody could ever get to it—not as punishment, but as protection. By keeping the Tree of Life safe from man, He was keeping man safe from eternal hell. It wasn't an angry and vindictive

Father who expected His children to act perfectly without making mistakes, but a Father who loved His children and wanted to keep the option for eternal life open when they were in a better condition to receive it.

In the end of the book of Revelation we see an invitation to finally come and partake of the Tree of Life. Why? Because Jesus came to remove the sin-consciousness and shame that was caused by sin. In the Garden God merely covered their shame, but they still had their sin. On the cross Jesus took away are shame and our sin. Now we're truly ready to partake of that Tree because we can do so without it throwing us into an eternal cycle of *self-condemnation.*

Was God disappointed in what happened in the Garden? I'm sure! Just as any father is when he gives his child instructions and warnings and the child gets hurt from disobedience. You're disappointed that they disobeyed, but not because they broke a rule; you're disappointed because the act of breaking the rule hurt them. So then you're not focused on the rule as much as the injury. And the response of your heart isn't to enforce the rule but to heal the wound.

What did Jesus come to do? Not to enforce the rules, but to heal the wounds of sin.

Christ came to heal the injury caused by the broken rule; to remove the sin-consciousness that was inherited through Adam. He didn't come to get us to amplify sin and call it humility. He surely doesn't get pleasure when people sit in church telling Him how wretched and naked they are, because it was that same consciousness and confession that destroyed our relationship with God to begin with! (Not to mention, you're amazing and none of that stuff is true... unless you really are sitting in church naked... in which case, that's a little weird...)

Sin Separates Us From God

Many have looked at Adam's banishment from the Garden and concluded that "Sin separates us from God!" And they believe that, to this day, when you sin God pushes you away at arms-length and turns His face from you until you ask Him to forgive you. That was how I perceived God all throughout the dark days I was trapped in sin. It made it that much more unbearable because I loved Him so much, but I hated that feeling of separation (and the idea that I would always have to experience it over and over until I died, since it was in my nature to keep sinning).

I often found myself with the same guilt and shame of Adam. If I sinned on a Sunday, I would often choose not to go to church. I would apologize to God and say, "I don't want you to see me like this!" and I believed He didn't want to see me like that either. He'd rather me just stay home than show up to church stained with filth.

Do I believe there was a separation in the Garden? Absolutely! But when I read the Garden story, it's clear that the separation wasn't on God's end. It was *man* who hid from *God*, it was never God who hid from man. Even after Adam sinned, God still approached Him for a conversation. God made no acknowledgment of Adam's sin until Adam acknowledged it first through the manifestation of his newfound knowledge—"I was afraid because I was naked."

Who taught you to be afraid of God and ashamed of yourself? It wasn't God. And so those confessions of fear and shame are not inspired by His Spirit.

God came into the Garden that day looking for His usual communion with His friend. But as soon as He realized that his friend's focus had shifted from *outward* to *inward*, He knew that the relationship was going to be different from then on out. Like any relationship where one person is more concerned with themself than the person they are in the relationship with, it doesn't last—it can't.

Scripture says that Jesus came to reconcile us to God. In order for there to be reconciliation there first has to be separation. So yes, I do believe that sin separates people from God, but I believe it only does that on man's end when man becomes more focused on his own sin and shame than he is on the fact that the God of the universe is still showing up to the Garden looking for a conversation, despite the disobedient act.

The Problem Occurs in the Mind

> "At one time you were separated from God. You were his enemies **in your minds**, because the evil you did was against him." – Col. 1:21 (ERV)

Were you His enemies in *His* mind because of your sin? No. It says you were His enemies in *your* minds because of your sin. Throughout scripture there are numerous times where God tries to approach the Israelites to have relationship with them, but because of how they perceived Him, they chose to stay hiding in the shadows rather than coming out into the light. Like Adam, they were afraid of God because of what *they* had done against Him. They saw firsthand what He could do (He drowned the entire Egyptian army to get them out of slavery), and from their perspective, who could survive in a relationship with God? Although they often spoke well of Him, it was often out of fear and obligation because to get on His bad side was to die. (Many in the church still relate to God this way.)

Hiding in Darkness

John mentioned this problem in the beginning of his gospel.

> *"He came into the very world he created, but the world didn't recognize him. He came to his own people, and even they rejected him." – John 1:10 (NLT)*

And later in the same book, Jesus says,

> *"This is the verdict: Light has come into the world, but people loved darkness instead of light because their deeds were evil." – John 3:10 (NLT)*

We as Christians read verses like that and think, "Yeah! People are so evil! People LOVE the darkness because they LOVE to sin!" But think about it for a second. Is that really what He's trying to get across? Is that the only possible way to interpret that verse? Is that what Adam did in the Garden? Did he seek the safety of the shadow because he wanted to continue sinning? Or did he seek it because he was ashamed of the sin he had already done? It wasn't the love of sin that caused Adam to hide, it was the shame caused by sin and the fear of how God would respond to it. The light exposed Adam's nakedness so he retreated to the shadows. Of course they loved the darkness of the tree they hid behind! Not because they were horribly wicked people who wanted to commit some more sin, but because the darkness of the tree made them feel safe. In their mind, it hid them and their shame from God, who they expected punishment from.

Let's look at this a different way. Is a child evil because they hide under the blankets when they think a monster is out to get them? No. They're hiding for safety. They think there is refuge under the blankets. "If I can't see the monster, the monster can't see me!" All through the Old Testament (and even still today) God is presented as an angry monster out to get people for their sin. So naturally, people are going to want to remain in the darkness, hoping to escape Him.

Someone will say, "You're watering down their sin!"

No. I'm not trying to "water down" their sin, I'm merely pointing out that the reason man hid from God in the first place was not because he wanted to continue sinning in the cloak of darkness, but because the darkness made him feel like his shame was hidden from God.

What the Pharisees did to the "sinners" of their day, a lot of people do to the "sinners" of our day. They run around trying to expose other people's sin. They think the best strategy for conversion is to throw the adulteress to the ground in the middle of the town square and tell everyone about her sin. "Look at what you did! Your evil deeds are brought to the light!" And that's precisely the reason people are hiding in darkness in the first place, because they don't want their shame to be exposed that way. Therefore it's probably not the best "conversion" tactic to run around embarrassing and shaming people over the sin that has already pushed them into the shadows. If you find out somebody is ashamed of their body, are you going to pull their pants down in public and humiliate them? (There's a reason it says the *Holy Spirit* convicts the world of sin. He can do so gently and privately without embarrassing the person and pushing them further into shame, which only results in more sin.)

People hid from God because they expected judgment and punishment for their evil deeds when their evil deeds were exposed. Many Christians today only reinforce that idea when they talk about God. But God isn't turning the lights on and exposing sin to embarrass us or use our bad deeds as leverage against us (as we'll see in the next chapter), instead He uncovers those things so he can then remove the shame of them from us entirely. Why does love cover a multitude of sins? For the very same reason God made animal skins to cover Adam's nakedness. It's to take our focus away from the shame and condemnation, not to make a bigger deal out of it in hopes that we will get scared of hell enough to reluctantly repeat a ritualistic prayer.

Think I'm full of it? Good! Don't take my word for it. But look at how Jesus ministered to "sinners." Look at how He talked to the Samaritan woman. He exposed her sin, yes, but He didn't embarrass her over it.

All through the Old Testament there is a perception in their minds that God is vindictive and angry at man because of sin. Jesus even said, "Nobody has seen God," meaning not every perception of God written in the Old Testament is true about Him. Remember, their perception of God was being filtered through a sin-corrupted mind, but our perception of God is filtered through the person of Jesus, who perfectly represented the Father.

I very much believe that there was a real separation between man and God after the fall. But again, I believe it was on the side of man as a result of how man's new self-centered, sin-conscious mind caused him to see God. That was the fatal blow.

Since the corrupted man only knows how to focus on himself, everything he believes about God has to first be filtered through that self-centeredness. The sin-corrupted mind, therefore, automatically attributes the negative aspects of itself to God and everything else it looks at. This is why God is often spoken of as a self-seeker out to gain glory for Himself at any cost (even if it means giving someone cancer or destroying an entire city), despite the fact that scripture says "God is love" and "Love is not self-seeking."

None of this is to say that there wasn't a real spiritual separation between man and God, or that it was merely a metaphor. Paul said that whoever has joined himself to the Lord is one Spirit with the Lord, just as a man who joins himself to a woman becomes one flesh with her.[2] The "becoming one" implies that they weren't one to begin with. Adam and Eve came from the same flesh, yes, but they weren't united into one flesh until a classic Marvin Gaye song came on and gave them some inspiration. There was a *real* separation between God and man. However, God became an enemy in our minds—in the way we looked at Him—He was never really out to get us. Still don't believe me? Good! Let's look at Jesus.

Endnotes

[1] See Philippians 2:3
[2] See 1 Cor. 6:17

Second Adam Reconciles Us

"For in him all the fullness of God was pleased to dwell, and through him to reconcile to himself all things, whether on earth or in heaven, making peace by the blood of his cross." (ERV)

Notice that He's not reconciling Himself to all things, but reconciling all things to Himself? It shows again that the separation wasn't on His end. If He were the one who had separated Himself from us then it would be our job to reconcile Him back to ourselves, rather than His job to reconcile us to Himself. Ironically, many do think it's their job to draw God closer through their repentance and confession of sin, rather than accepting that He has already brought them closer to Himself.

Christ wasn't making peace with God on behalf of man, He was making peace with man on behalf of God. It was man's mind that was hostile towards God to begin with. The whole creation became frustrated because of the curse of sin, but Christ reconciled every hostile thing, whether on earth or in heaven, to Himself.[1] He made peace where there had only been war.

His repentance message wasn't, "Repent! For the wrath of God is at hand!" but rather, "Repent! For the Kingdom of God is at hand." His ministry wasn't to turn people away from their sin and save them from God's wrath towards man, but to turn man's hostile mind back to a right perspective of God, and save them from their own wrath against Him (and the crucifixion is the perfect illustration of just how hostile we were towards Him).

In changing our perspective to better understand our Father, sin is naturally turned away from without sin having to be the forceful emphasis. Jesus said that eternal life is to know the one true God, and the One He sent. Eternal life doesn't come through turning away from sin, but from knowing God, who is perfectly seen through Jesus.

It was our minds that needed to be renewed and changed. Coincidentally, the word "repent" simply means "change your mind."[2] Paul said "be transformed by" what? Renewing your mind.[3] Renovate the old, and make it new again.[4] This is what Jesus came to do by showing us the Father we only get glimpses of in the Old Testament.

The Perfect Image of God

Everything Jesus did in His life and ministry was opposite to the God we see in the Old Testament. The God in the Old Testament would have never hesitated to have the adulteress stoned (in fact, that's the reason they thought she should be stoned in the first place). But Jesus said, "I do not condemn you, go and sin no more."[5]

Does this mean the Old Testament God was *different*? Or that the Son was at odds with the Father? *Not at all!* It was the perception of God that was different, and Christ was changing that old perception from "God is an angry judge who must punish sinners!" to "God is patient and full of mercy, not wanting anyone to perish. His will for the creation is simply, 'Be whole again!'"

Why do we think Jesus didn't treat "sinners" like the religious leaders of His day did, who believed God was angry and judgmental? He went to parties with drunks and prostitutes, for crying out loud! Do we think He was just trying to butter them up for conversion so He could sneak in an invitation for the "sinner's prayer"? No. It was God in Christ saying, "I'm not the person they told you I am. I'm not angry at you over sin, I'm angry at sin over you. And now I'm about to deal with that problem once and for all!"

Jesus came to "take away the sin of the world," not because sin kept God from getting to us, but because it kept us from getting to God. He has pursued us (not run from us) ever since the fall, but we could never respond to Him because our minds were hostile towards Him (no matter how good we spoke of Him). But in Christ taking away the sin of the world, His goal was to remove that hostile perception of our Father so we could see Him as He truly is. Now we see the Father through the crystal clear lens of the Son, rather than the dirty lens of our own self-centered sin nature.

> "Or do you presume on the riches of his kindness and forbearance and patience, not knowing that God's kindness is meant to lead you to repentance?" – Romans 2:4 (ERV)

His kindness is meant to lead us to a change of mind (repentance). What is He leading us to change our mind about? About *Him*! That we would no longer see the angry man-destroyer of the Old Testament who must always get His retribution, but now, as revealed through Christ—the visible image of the invisible God— we receive the *proper* perception of God. The one who is not willing that *anyone* should perish, but that all would come to repentance;

who longs for that uncorrupted relationship He had with man in the Garden.[6]

The Message of Reconciliation

*"All this is from God, who through Christ reconciled us to himself and gave us the ministry of reconciliation; that is, in Christ God was reconciling the world to himself, **not counting their trespasses against them**, and entrusting to us the message of reconciliation." – 2 Cor.5:18-19 (ERV)*

- What is the message He has entrusted to us? "The message of reconciliation."
- What is the message of reconciliation? That, in Christ, God was reconciling the world to Himself, **not counting their sins against them**.

Our message is of His kindness and *refusal* to hold men's sin against them, not of His anxiousness to destroy cities and people because of their sin. Jesus even rebuked His own disciples when they thought they should call down judgment and fire on the people that rejected Him.[7]

Your sinful actions aren't the issue; your perspective is. This may upset many people. Saying things like this has caused many to accuse me of being soft on sin (or even endorsing it) because I make a bigger deal of God's kindness and patience than I do of anger and judgment (as if it's out of line to believe that "mercy triumphs over judgment"). We're not "soft on sin," we're soft on people despite their sin, just as Christ was soft on us "while we were yet sinners."

"God demonstrates His own love for us in this: While we were still sinners Christ died for us." – Romans 5:8 (NIV)

That's another one of those verses we love to quote, but many only seem to want to take it seriously when it's in regards to their own sin. When it's in regards to other people's sin (especially those of opposing political or religious views) then God's wrath must be emphasized! *No mercy! Now is the time for judgment!* We don't mind when others are punished for their sin—in fact, sometimes we ruthlessly demand it—but when it comes time for us to pay the piper for our own (or at least we believe it's that time), you can bet we're pleading the blood of Jesus and proclaiming God's unconditional love and forgiveness every which way we can.

We see the same thing throughout the Old Testament as the judges and prophets pronounced mercy and forgiveness over themselves and their own people (Israel)—God was always spoken of as this guy who was slow to anger and quick to forgive—but when it came to other camps (pagans and non-Jewish people), you can be sure He had His chariots of fire lined up on the frontlines ready for war, and forgiveness was a foreign term.

Scripture says, "Mercy triumphs over judgment." That's what we see this in the life of Jesus.[8] The only harsh judgment we see Him showing is towards the religious judges who were condemning the people He came to save. It wasn't because He didn't love the Pharisees, but because they were perpetuating the old idea that God is a sin-focused boogeyman out to get anyone who didn't behave perfectly (except for them, of course!). Jesus was there to show people the exact opposite view of God.

Jesus Did More Than We Know

One of the biggest cop outs I've heard from Christians regarding sin is, "Well, we live in a fallen world." What they mean is that, even though we're not of this world, we live in this world, so we're always going to be affected by the fall of this world (meaning, we're always going to sin). The person who says that doesn't realize that Jesus took away our inheritance in Adam (sin, death, sickness, disease, etc.) and gave us His inheritance (we'll talk about this throughout the rest of the book). How can I be bound to the effects of Adam's fall when I have been completely removed from Adam altogether?

We often diminish the work of Christ and think He only came to bring forgiveness of sins, when He came to do so much more. He came to forgive sins, yes, but He also came to take away the sin of the world (John 1:29). He also came to destroy the devil's work (which in context is speaking of sin and every negative effect), and heal everyone who was oppressed by the devil (1 John 3:8, Acts 10:38). He also came to kill our sinful selves and give us new lives based in His righteousness (Romans 6, 2 Cor. 5:21). He also came to show us *exactly* what God looks like (John 14:9, Col. 1:15, Heb. 1:3), what humanity is destined to look like (Romans 8:29), and much more.

A Recap

The sin nature turned our mind towards ourselves and our actions. Through that it turned our focus to sin and shame and caused our mind to become hostile towards God, because we constantly expected punishment and judgment. As a result, we instinctively tried to hide from Him in order to preserve our lives.

It's hard for a woman to have a proper relationship with an abusive husband. She may still do the things he tells her to do, but it's done out of fear that he will hurt her if she doesn't go along with everything he demands. It can't be a healthy relationship because it's one where action and obedience are influenced by fear, not love (though if somebody asks, *of course she loves her husband*! She has to or he will black her eyes, or maybe worse).

In the same way, we couldn't have real relationship with God because we lived in constant fear of Him. Our perception of Him was corrupt. This is how we see mankind relating to God throughout the Old Testament. Man didn't see God as a faithful husband or a loving Father, but as a wife-beater and child-abuser. He was terrifying. But the gospel (good news) is that Jesus reconciled us to God and gave us a clear understanding of who He really is: not an angry judge out for revenge, but a loving Father out for restoration.

God isn't Angry at You

Although it might sound like I've bunny trailed, I'm telling you these things because I want you to know that God isn't holding a single one of your sins against you. Should you go and sin immediately after reading this book, God isn't holding it against you, neither is He tapping His foot and shaking His finger at you. Is that me saying you *should* go sin? Not at all! It's me saying you have no excuse to because not only has He forgiven your sin, not only has He decided to never remember your sin or hold it against you, but He has also taken your sin away, and the part of you that used to gravitate towards sin is dead. So how can you continue living that way?

It's His kindness and refusal to punish us that's meant to lead us to repentance (a change of mind) about how He sees us, resulting in a change in how we see Him. Now I can boldly approach His throne (come in close for a real relationship) without the fear of dying. How could I ever go back to those chains when He has set me free? Why would I ever want to look for a reason to continue doing the things I was incapable of avoiding before?

When you know how He sees you and what He has given you, it will empower you to live free, just as those who believe God sees them as filthy wretches trapped in sin continue to live as though it's true. It's the perspective of the heart that needs changing, not the behavior of the person. Behavior will happen on its own when the heart is changed to see what He sees. Stop believing you're a sinner with a sin nature. Change your mind and watch how quickly everything else changes as a result.

How much has the modern definition of "repentance" (getting sad and feeling guilty over your sin) actually helped you to stop sinning? If it did, I don't think you would be reading a book titled How to Overcome Sin, since you would already know that the answer to that question is to verbally flog yourself in the dark while the worship band plays the latest contemporary Christian hit.

Endnotes

[1] See Rom. 8:19-21

[2] G3340, Strong's Concordance

[3] Webster's Definition: Renew

[4] G342, Strong's Concordance

[5] See John 8:11

[6] I'm aware that the verses surrounding Romans 2:4 are about judgment. But as is the point I am making in this section, the judgment of the self-centered man is based on entitlement and revenge ("Eye for an eye!"), but Christ never showed that vengeful attitude towards people over sin. We often like to think our idea of judgment is God's idea of judgment, but our idea of judgment is often based on that Old Testament perception of God, who was never a clear depiction of who God really is.

[7] See Luke 9:51-55

[8] See James 2:13

The New Creation

Romans 8:29 says that we were predestined to be conformed to the likeness of Christ. What does that mean? Same thing it means in Genesis when God said, "Let us create man in our image." We were made to resemble Him.

Many think the "process of sanctification" is a transformation from rotten human into glorious saint that will only be completed through death (and they are right, but remember Romans 6? We already died), but according to scripture, we're already like Jesus is, we're only learning how to walk it out.[1]

We were created in His image, but we're still learning what that image looks like as we grow in relationship and continue getting to know Him.[2] Jesus is what humanity looks like at its full potential. However, Paul says elsewhere that we're growing up into Christ. Understandably then, we're not going to fulfill that potential perfectly all the time (not right away, anyway),[3] but I do like to believe that as we grow and get to know Him, it's absolutely possible for us to fulfill that potential in our lifetime.

Laying Down False Humility

Avoiding sin isn't what makes you holy; knowing you're holy is what makes you avoid sin. Holy people don't sin, sinners sin, so if you believe yourself to be a sinner who will always be prone to sin, then you will always find yourself stuck in sin. You're only fulfilling the actions of the type of person you believe yourself to be.

Since I know I'm made in the image of Christ, not only that, but I was created to be conformed to His likeness (that is to adapt to it), I know that it's possible to live sin free just as He did.

"So you're saying you're Jesus?"

Not at all! I don't have a beard.

What I'm saying is that I'm like Him (so are you). He's the blueprint that humanity is based on, and He's what humanity looks like when it's in full working order. If that's offensive to you because you think it's offensive to God, I can assure you that if God was offended by the idea of man being like Him, He never would have said, "Let us create man in our image."

A lot of people don't want to deal with that idea because their behavior doesn't line up with it, and they think that such a holy and perfect God is disgusted by the idea of a filthy human saying they are "like Him." They'd rather trust what their behavior tells them, rather than what scripture tells them. They think it's humble to say, "I can never be like Him!" when God has said, "Too late! You already are!"

Do you remember what happened when Jesus claimed to be God's son? It was more offensive to the religious crowd than anything He had done or said prior. He said, "I and the Father are one," and they instantly picked up stones to stone Him.[4]

Religion glories in the separation of man and God. It loves to emphasize distance so it can show how great its own efforts are to close the gap. But Jesus said, "There's no gap, no distance, and no separation. I and the Father are one."

Is that offensive? You bet! Enough to get you crucified. But it didn't stop Jesus from saying it, or from later praying in the garden *"that they may be one as we are one—I in them and you in me."*[5] Did Jesus get what He prayed for? Paul seemed to think so when he told the Corinthians they were one Spirit with the Lord![6]

Contrary to popular opinion, humanity doesn't gross God out. If it did, He would have never taken on its "filthy" flesh. True humility is agreeing with what God says about you, not resisting it. It doesn't matter if your behavior has not yet lined up with what He says, agree with Him anyways because He probably knows what He's talking about better than you or I!

What You Believe Determines What You Do

By putting your faith in the idea that you're a filthy human whose nature it is to sin, you're subconsciously making sin the natural thing to do. However, if you put faith in holiness then you will be consumed by holiness, because you'll know that sinning is contrary to who you are in Christ.

Does that mean you'll lose your ability to sin? No. Adam sinned without a sin nature, we can too. But the more wrapped up we are in who we are in Christ, the less likely we are to do things that are contrary to His character.

If I believe I'm a sinner, then it's less likely I'm going to give myself over to holy behavior. On the contrary, if I believe I'm holy, then it's less likely I'm going to give myself to sinful behavior. Why? Because with a sin nature I have to try *not* to sin (though I can never succeed because that nature controls me), but with a holy nature I have to try *to* sin, since sin now becomes the unnatural thing to do, and I realize it's an actual choice (I control it). I'm not "prone to sin," I'm prone to do the good works I was created in Christ to do.[7]

Holiness vs. Sinfulness

In 1 Peter 1:14-16 it says, "Be holy because I am holy." Notice that it doesn't say, "Become holy because I am holy."

You're already holy, but you're learning what it looks like to be.[8] Consequently, living holy is the natural way for you to live. It's not meant to be this horrible struggle, trying to make yourself more Christ-like. You are as Christ-like as you're ever going to get; maybe not in behavior yet, but the behavior follows the belief.

Let's look at the rest of the verse.

> *"As obedient children, do not conform to the evil desires you had when you lived in ignorance. But just as he who called you is holy, so be holy in all you do; for it is written: "Be holy, because I am holy."*
> *(NIV)*

The implication here is that they didn't currently have evil desires. Why do I say that? Look at what Peter says next.

> *"Do not conform to the evil desires you...**had**...when you...**lived**...in ignorance."*

See the past-tense? He didn't say that they currently have evil desires and they must pray and fast for God to cleanse their wickedness and make them holy.[9] He said that when they used to live in ignorance of God, they...**had**...evil desires. If he's telling you not to let it happen, that means you have way more control over it than you realize.

You're Brand New!

Understand that when you were an old creation, you did have evil desires, you did have a sinful nature, and your mind was hostile towards God. But now you're a new creation in Christ—"Behold! All things have become new."[10]

The word "new" there in the Greek is "kainos."[11] It's not talking about being refurbished or repaired. When it says you're a new creation, and that all things have become new, it's saying that you have been freshly created, and all things are, in the most literal sense, brand new... as in they've never been seen before in the history of the world.

When the Xbox first came out, it had never been seen before. Yes, there were many other videogame consoles on the market, and they had been around for years, but 2001 marked the first time in history that we ever saw a game console from Microsoft. It was never heard of before. Likewise, while there had already been humans for thousands of years before Jesus came, His arrival on Earth marked the first time in our planet's history that we saw a cross-species of God and man. It was such an offensive idea to the people in Jesus' day that they had Him killed. But from then on out, whoever received Him was given new life, reborn and made like Him.

Not only was Jesus the "last Adam," but He was also the firstborn of the new Creation. He died as the last human being, and raised as the firstborn of the new creation. Where are you? On the new creation side, not on the Adam side. How do we know? Because Jesus was the "last Adam."

We're no longer part of the old species that looked for God in buildings and temples, now we have become the buildings and temples where God is found. Before Jesus, that had never been seen before. Nobody in the Old Testament could even comprehend it. It's the great mystery that Paul talked about that was kept hidden for ages past, but has now been revealed to the saints (that's you!).[12]

You're not that same being that descended from Adam. You're now a being that has descended directly from God. Just as Christ wasn't born through two humans, but was conceived through the Holy Spirit, so you too have also been recreated anew, conceived through the Holy Spirit. You're not figuratively God's child, but in this new creation life He is your actual birth dad. Adam is no longer at the head of your bloodline, the Creator of the Universe is.

That's what scripture means when it calls Christ "the firstborn of many brethren."[13] He was the first of the new species to be a direct descendent of God through the Holy Spirit, not through human reproduction.[14]

John made this clear.

> "But some people did accept him. They believed in him, and he gave them the right to become children of God. They became God's children, but not in the way babies are usually born. It was not because of any human desire or plan. They were born from God himself." - John 1:12-13 (ERV)

Jesus also made it just as clear to Nicodemus.

> "Very truly I tell you, no one can see the kingdom of God unless they are born again."
>
> "How can someone be born when they are old?" Nicodemus asked. "Surely they cannot enter a second time into their mother's womb to be born!"
>
> Jesus answered, "Very truly I tell you, no one can enter the kingdom of God unless they are born of water and the Spirit. Flesh gives birth to flesh, but the Spirit gives birth to spirit. You should not be surprised at my saying, 'You must be born again.' – John 3:3-7 (NIV)

"Born again" means that the person that existed before the "again" is gone. That's why you need the "again." If you died with Christ, but were never "born again," you would just be dead. But since you died, then you were reborn (raised to new life with Christ, birthed by the Spirit and now living in the Spirit), you are now alive as a brand new person. What does "rebirth" mean? It means the first birth no longer counts. It's been "forgiven," (or in other words, "dismissed from mind").[15]

Adam Ain't Your Daddy No More!

Many still live under the idea that they have evil desires, when they don't. They think they're still connected to Adam when they're not. We all know the routine: because of Adam, we were all born into a depraved and sinful life. From the time of Adam's sin, all of humanity was plunged into darkness and became wicked and full of evil desires. It's true. That really did happen! However, the person you were who was a descendant of Adam, died.

All of those scriptures about dying with Christ, and about how you "no longer live," they're not just some buttery spiritual fluff metaphors for us to quote so we can experience temporary relief in the momentary forgetfulness of our failures. They're telling us over and over that the old person that we were who inherited the curse of sin and death through Adam's humanity, is dead—they're never coming back—but this new person has inherited the blessing of life and freedom through Christ.

> "Those who belong to Christ Jesus have crucified their sinful self. They have given up their old selfish feelings and the evil things they wanted to do." - Galatians 5:24 (ERV)

> *"When you came to Christ, you were "circumcised," but not by a physical procedure. Christ performed a spiritual circumcision—the cutting away of your sinful nature."- Col. 2:11 (NLT)*

It doesn't mean you've lost your ability to think and do bad things—you still have the responsibility to manage your thoughts and actions—but, your true nature is to have a mind set on the things above, because you have the mind of Christ.[16] You do have to learn to manage your thoughts, but you already have everything needed to do so, therefore it's not the same work-yourself-up routine that we've been taught to do in order to get sin out of our life.[17]

Sin is not the issue, unbelief is. We have failed to believe that when scripture says Jesus took away the sin of the world, it really means it. We find all kinds of ways around it because, undeniably, Christians still sin! But what if they only continue to sin, not because they are wicked, but because they've not believed the good news that He took their sin away?

What happens when you believe? Well, since holy is who I am, holiness itself becomes the natural way to live. However, like anything else, it takes practice. It takes changing your mind, and it takes a lot of grace and patience with yourself as you learn and grow into the full stature of Jesus.

A Lesson from Babies

Would you yell at a baby for falling when they're learning how to walk? I hope not. Is that baby any less human because it falls? No. Like little babies we are learning how to walk, and eventually we'll have it figured out. In the meantime, you're no less Christian because you fall, just understand that you're learning, and one day you will be so good at walking that falling won't even cross your mind. God forbid we continue believing the lie that we'll never learn to walk until we die!

Give yourself grace to fall. And if you do fall, learn from it and do better next time. Babies don't fall and then curse themselves for it.

"Dad, I'm such a wretched baby who is prone to falling!"

Instead, they figure out why they fell, and correct for the next time they try. If they fall again, they examine what went wrong that time, and correct again. On and on until pretty soon that baby is running all over the house, nearly impossible to catch. Trying to avoid falling no longer even crosses their mind because walking has become natural, and now they're having so much fun running.

If you punished a baby every time they fell, they might just lose the will to learn how to walk, since if they don't get everything right the first time, they get into loads of trouble. If we were to treat children that way, we would take away every opportunity they have to grow. That's not how God wants us to live. That's not how God treats us when we fall.

Endnotes

[1] See John 4:17

[2] See Gen. 1:26

[3] See Eph. 4:13

[4] See John 10:29-33

[5] See John 17:20-23

[6] 1 Cor. 6:17

[7] See Eph. 2:10

[8] See Heb. 10:10. You are already holy because of what Jesus did.

[9] See John 15:3. You are already clean because of what Jesus did.

[10] See 2 Cor. 5:17, Col. 1:21-23. You were once enemies of God in your mind because of your actions (the same way Adam's perspective of God changed after he sinned). But God has reconciled you to Himself through what Jesus did, and now presents you to Himself holy, blameless and without anything that would make you guilty. The guilt of Adam that swallowed up humanity and made our minds and actions hostile towards God has been destroyed. We've been reconciled, and relationship has been restored.

[11] G2537, Strong's Concordance

[12] See Col. 1:27

[13] See Rom. 8:29

[14] Note that I'm not denying His divinity

[15] From Thesaurus.com

[16] See 1 Cor. 2:16

[17] See Eph. 1:3, 2 Peter 1:3, Titus 2:11-12

What About 1 John?

"What about 1 John 1?"

This is probably the most popular question people ask in response to the claim that we can live sin free.

> "'If we say we have not sinned, we make him a liar, and his word is not in us.' So if you're saying you can live without sinning, God's word isn't in you!"[1]

Sometimes I feel like people enjoy thinking of themselves as sinners *way too much*!

First, we need to understand that in this letter, John is attempting to deal with an idea called Gnosticism that had crept into the church. There are many details we could go into about Gnosticism, and I encourage you to look into it on your own so you can better understand John's letter, but for now we'll just talk about the basics.

The Gnostics believed the material world (including the flesh) was evil, and the spiritual world was good. In that, they believed that it was impossible for God, who is spirit and good, to become flesh.

Therefore they denied that Jesus actually came in the flesh, and instead concluded that He was only an illusion. We see this in the introduction of 1 John as he tries to make it abundantly clear to them, "We have seen Jesus with our eyes and touched him with our hands." He's letting them know that Jesus wasn't a ghost, or an illusion, but He did in fact have a physical body, and there were plenty of people who could testify about it. The Gnostics also denied that sin was real, and wrote that off as an illusion as well. This is the perspective which John is attempting to counter.

> "That which was from the beginning, which we have heard, which we have seen with our eyes, which we have looked at and our hands have touched—this we proclaim concerning the Word of life. The life appeared; we have seen it and testify to it, and we proclaim to you the eternal life, which was with the Father and has appeared to us. We proclaim to you what we have seen and heard, so that you also may have fellowship with us. And our fellowship is with the Father and with his Son, Jesus Christ. We write this to make our joy complete." – 1 John 1:1-4 (NIV)

Here we see John introducing his letter and informing his audience that Jesus was a real person, by confirming that he had seen Jesus with his own eyes, and touched Him with his own hands. Why is he proclaiming that Jesus came in the flesh? "...so that you also may have fellowship with us." What's the implication there? That they didn't already have fellowship with them. And if they aren't in fellowship with the believers, what does that make them? Unbelievers. What does that mean? 1 John 1 is written to unbelievers. Although the Gnostics considered themselves to be Christians, by the Christian standard (the requirement that you actually have faith in Jesus), they were not (they thought salvation came through attaining a certain level of enlightenment and knowledge, not through the work of Jesus). This is important to understand when you read this letter.

> *"This is the message we have heard from him and declare to you: God is light; in him there is no darkness at all." (1:5)*

Right here he is setting up the beginning of his altar call. What I mean is that he's aiming this explanation of the gospel at the unbelievers in the crowd, not the believers (just like many pastors do at the end of their church sermons when they change their focus to a different audience). How do we know he's not talking to the believers? Because the believers would have already heard and believed this message.

> *"This is the message we have heard from him and declare to you: God is light; in him there is no darkness at all. If we claim to have fellowship with him and yet walk in the darkness, we lie and do not live out the truth. But if we walk in the light, as he is in the light, we have fellowship with one another, and the blood of Jesus, his Son, purifies us from all sin." (1:5-7)*

The Gnostics were claiming to have fellowship with Jesus, but they didn't believe that He had actually came in the flesh to save them from their sins (again, they believed both the physical manifestation of Jesus and sin were illusions). Therefore, although they were claiming to have fellowship with Christ, they were actually walking in the darkness and not living out the truth. They weren't walking in the light, and they didn't "have fellowship with one another." (We know this because John just said, "We proclaim to you… so that you will have fellowship with us.")

> *"If we claim to be without sin, we deceive ourselves and the truth is not in us."* – 1:8

Why does he say this? Not to say "you'll never live free from sin! You're always going to sin until you die," but to counter the Gnostic belief that sin is an illusion. Since they believed it was an illusion, they claimed to be without it. And since they claimed to be without it, they didn't believe there was anything for Jesus to purify them from. So John is saying, "Listen. You can't say you're walking in truth (that you know Jesus), and then claim that you don't have sin. If you claim to be without sin, you deceive yourselves and the truth (Jesus) is not in you."

> "If we confess our sins, he is faithful and just and will forgive us our sins and purify us from all unrighteousness." (1:9)

He isn't saying to the Christian, "God will only forgive you of your sin if you confess each one of your sins! Make sure to keep a long record of every bad thing you do so you can tell God about it (even though 'God is love' and 'love keeps no record of wrongs'), otherwise He won't forgive you!" He's still talking to the Gnostics (the technically non-believer) and continuing from the previous sentence.

"If you say you don't have sin, you deceive yourselves and the truth is not in you. [But] If you confess your sins, he is faithful and just and will forgive your sins and purify you from all unrighteousness. If you claim you have not sinned [as the Gnostics did], you make him out to be a liar and his word is not in you."

Did you notice I changed the word "we" to "you"? I did so because John is using the term "we" here in a general sense to refer to them, just as I have throughout this book. He's not saying "we" in the sense of himself or other Christians, but in the sense of that group of unbelievers. Now he switches focus and begins talking to the Christians.

> "My dear children, I write this to you so that you will not sin." 1 John 2:1 (NIV)

Now, how is it possible that he is writing this so that they will not sin, if they are always damned and destined to sin for the rest of their lives? It would make no sense for me to write something with the hope that you won't do something, when I know you're always going to do it. It would even be cruel for me to send you a letter that implies the possibility that you won't do it, even though it's impossible for you to avoid it.

So John is writing them so that they will not sin...

> *"But if anybody does sin, we have an advocate with the Father—Jesus Christ, the Righteous One."*

"But when anybody does sin"—oh wait! Back up. It doesn't say *when*, it says *if*. What is an 'if'? It's the opposite of a guarantee. The Greek word here is "ean," the definition meaning "if, in case."

John doesn't give a guarantee that you will sin, in fact, he says he's writing with the hope that you won't sin, meaning he actually believes it's possible to not sin (that heretic!). To confirm this, we can jump forward to Chapter 3, where he makes it incredibly clear that we're not to continue sinning if we are believers.

To Take Away our Sins

> *"But you know that he appeared so that he might take away our sins. And in him is no sin. No one who lives in him keeps on sinning. No one who continues to sin has either seen him or known him." – 1 John 3:5-6 (NIV)*

Where are our sins? Swept under the carpet? "Covered" by His blood? No. Our sins have been "taken away." They've been removed. They're not hidden, or covered, or buried, or painted over with the blood of Jesus, but by the blood of Jesus our sins are taken away and forgotten!

"And in Him is no sin."

Where are you? In Him.

Where is sin? Not in Him.

If you are in Him, and there is no sin in Him, then is it safe to say that there is no sin in you? Yes!

> *"No one who lives in him keeps on sinning. No one who continues to sin has either seen him or known him." – 3:6*

This is a big claim, and a very uncomfortable one at that, depending on how you read it. At first, it almost sounds like he's saying if you're not immediately a perfect person upon conversion, then you must not really be saved! But I don't think that's what he's saying (this is the Apostle of Love after all!), and we can see in his language ("dear children") that he isn't preaching hell fire and condemnation on them. Instead, the context of this section is about how Jesus came to take away our sin, therefore if we truly believe in that like we say, how can we continue sinning? It's the same thing Paul said in Romans 6:1-2, "If we're dead to sin, how can we live in it any longer?"

Now don't start feeling condemned on me! I'm not implying that you're not saved if you've sinned since becoming a Christian. After all, they don't generally teach us these kinds of things in church. It's really not our fault if we continued sinning after becoming a Christian when we've practically been taught that it's the normal thing to do until we die. However, scripture doesn't teach that.

> *"Dear children, do not let anyone lead you astray. The one who does what is right is righteous, just as he is righteous. [8] The one who does what is sinful is of the devil, because the devil has been sinning from the beginning." – (3:7-8)*

Remember, he's still on the topic of sin, in the context of a letter written to confront Gnosticism and keep the believers on track. And he's in the middle of telling them that their sin has been taken away. Taking that into consideration, he's warning them not to be led astray in regards to what happened to their sin. Don't let anyone tell you that sin is an illusion, and therefore Jesus didn't actually take it away.

I would repeat this warning to you today. Don't let anyone lead you astray regarding what Christ did with our sin. He took it away, forever disconnecting us from it. We aren't still hopelessly attached to it, waiting to die so we can finally be rid of that misery. He has already dealt with the problem, now we're free to live apart from that horrible circle of hell.

> The one who does what is right is righteous, just as he is righteous. 8The one who does what is sinful is of the devil, because the devil has been sinning from the beginning." (3:7)

Is he saying here that you are righteous if you do good? No. We've already seen over and over in scripture that righteousness is not attained through your good behavior. So the "does what is right" part isn't saying that your righteousness is conditional on whether you do right, but rather that doing right is a reflection of your righteousness.

For example, if I see someone hold the door for an old lady and I think, "Wow. He's kind!" am I saying that he just attained kindness by his action? Or that the kindness he already has is being displayed through the action? The latter. In the same way, the person who does right is shown to be righteous, just as He is righteous.

If John were saying that "he who does what is righteous becomes righteous," then we have only come full circle into the vicious cycle of rule-keeping; and I hope I've already shown you how that turns out for anyone caught up in it.

> "The reason the Son of God appeared was to destroy the devil's work." (3:8)

What's the context, again? It's sin. So when John says Jesus came to destroy the devil's work, what is he referring to? Sin. So what happened to sin? It has been destroyed. What does that mean for you? You're free. How can you still be controlled by something that has been destroyed?

> *"No one who is born of God will continue to sin, because God's seed remains in them; they cannot go on sinning, because they have been born of God."* *(3:9)*

I don't know if John could be much clearer than he was here. If you are born of God, you *cannot go on sinning*. People find a lot of ways to wiggle out of this one since they have quite clearly gone on sinning after becoming a Christian, so instead of accepting the possibility that maybe we got it wrong, we have to conclude that John must have meant something else.

Does that verse mean they aren't really born of God? No. For one, we've been taught for generations that sinning is normal, and it should be expected. We're told that we have a sinful nature, a wicked heart, and we're just all around dirt bags that Jesus came to take pity on with salvation. The fact that we have continued sinning shouldn't be surprising to anyone—we've been taught to sin.

Our continued sin shouldn't be an indicator that we don't really know God. The fact of the matter is, no matter how much a Christian believes they're a wretched sinner who's prone to sin, they still have the desire to live free from sin. Whether they believe they can or not, they still desire to. This should be such a big sign that we're not as evil and wicked as we think. If we were really such wretches and sinners, then we shouldn't feel so horrible when we do the things wretches and sinners do.

"Well, that's just the Holy Spirit in me, grieved over my sin!"

But Holy Spirit is one with you, so it wouldn't be just Him who is grieved over your sin. Don't think of yourself and Him as two separate beings housed in the same body. You are both one Spirit. Speak like it. Live like it. That alone will begin to change your life dramatically.

So why do we go on sinning if we cannot go on sinning? The next chapter is all about that!

Endnotes

[1] See 1 John 1:10

Why Do We Still Sin?

The obvious question through all of this is, "If it's true that we're free from sin, and we can live without sinning, why do we still sin?" Many ask themselves that question, but since they don't immediately become sinless in their behavior, they conclude that all of those verses that blatantly say we're free from sin must mean something else. And anyone who says they can live sin free must be a heretic and a liar.

A lot of close friends got upset with me when I first started telling them these things. Some even decided it was good enough reason to quit speaking to me entirely. They were offended by the implications that we can live sin free, because they couldn't ever see it being a reality in this life since their own actions seemed so far from it. They were so focused on the fact that they have sinned every day since becoming a Christian, and believed so much that they were prone to it, that stopping anytime soon just wasn't a likely scenario. *If we could quit sinning, what would we need Jesus for?*

Coincidentally, after my mom finished reading my first book, she asked me this very question. "I finished your book, and I really liked it. But I have some questions. Are we only forgiven for our sins, or are we free from sin?" What she was asking me was whether Jesus died so we could be forgiven of our sins from now on (from the point of the cross forward)? Or did He die so we could stop sinning altogether?

I felt the excitement bubbling up in my chest as I waited for her to finish her question. I couldn't wait to say, "The answer is both!" Yes, Jesus died for the forgiveness of our sins, but also to set us free from sin altogether. In fact, the two go hand-in-hand. It's His forgiveness that empowers us to leave our life of sin. Just as Romans 2:4 says it's the kindness of God that leads us to repentance, and just as Jesus said in John 8:11, "I do not condemn you, go and sin no more!" A lot of people give others the "go and sin no more" command, but they fail to include the "I do not condemn you" part which is what empowers the person to go and sin no more. (We talked about how God's kindness leads to repentance in Chapter 7.)

Then what's the problem? If this is true, why do we still sin?

Clip, Clip!

While I was having this conversation with my mom, trying to explain our freedom from sin, I saw a pair of nail clippers sitting on my desk. Immediately I realized that even after receiving those nail clippers as a gift from my friend, I had still found myself biting my nails. The issue wasn't that I was just a no good "nail biter saved by grace," or that I will always be "prone to nail biting" until I die, but that I've been biting my nails for my entire life. There has been a lifelong habit formed around biting my nails, and it will drive me crazy if I expect those habits to change overnight. I'll feel like a horrible failure every time I catch myself biting my nails, because I know I shouldn't be doing that anymore.

The old habit of nail biting was made based on the fact that I've never owned a pair of nail clippers. Since it was my first nature for so long to bite my nails whenever I felt a sharp edge on them, it meant I would have to reprogram my mind (repent) and make my new first nature—my new habit—to grab the nail clippers whenever I needed to trim my nails.

In the same way, although our old sinful self has died on the cross with Christ—it is forever extinct—we still have old habits that were made while that old person was alive. So then we are "being transformed by the renewing of our mind." We are consciously forming new habits in place of those old ones, yet, in the meantime we might still occasionally catch ourselves falling into those old habits.

Do I feel guilty and ashamed whenever I catch myself biting my nails? Not at all! I just remind myself, "I have nail clippers right in front of me! Why would I bite my nails?" and then I grab those nail clippers and proceed to cut them. I have no reason to bite my nails because I now have a tool that is better designed to deal with the issue.

In the same way, I don't feel guilty and ashamed whenever I catch myself in sinful behavior (*gasp!*). I just remind myself, "I'm free from sin. I don't have that nature anymore. Why would I continue acting that way?" What am I doing? I'm renewing my mind. I'm staying conscious of the fact that the old has passed away and the new has come. I no longer need to act like I did in the old, because everything I've been given in the new enables me to live FREE. However, if I automatically expect all of my actions to change overnight, not only am I removing the process of growth, through which we gain wisdom and knowledge that helps others, I'm also going to find myself extremely disappointed, because I am growing, and growing includes messing up.

Grace is Enough

For a few days after I received those nail clippers, I still caught myself biting my nails. At first I would bite the nails on two or three fingers before I remembered I had nail clippers; the next time I would get about one; then half of one, then I got to a point where I would remember I had nail clippers as soon as I felt the urge to bite them, and finally, now the urge to bite them is gone, replaced by an cut them properly with the clippers. I didn't get angry at myself for biting my nails, I only reminded myself that I don't need to do that anymore.

I have grace and mercy on myself just as He has grace and mercy on me. Since I know that He doesn't condemn me when I sin, or get angry and disappointed at me and expect me to get everything right the first time, I'm able to treat myself with that same mercy and grace. I don't feel the need to verbally flog myself in front of Him to show Him how sorry I am for my mess-ups—He already knows. More importantly, He knows how much I desire to learn from Him so I can live up to my full potential in Him—not because the rules say I should behave better, but because I have a genuine desire to be like Him.

Therefore, He doesn't act like an abusive father who insults me and whips me with a belt because I messed up in the midst of trying to learn, rather He acts like the gracious Father and Teacher that He is, and He shows me where I messed up and how I can improve next time. He's not trying to make me feel guilty and condemned, instead He's trying to make me feel safe around Him.

If I lie, He doesn't rub the Ten Commandments in my face and say, "YOU SHOULDN'T LIE!" Yeah, thanks! I already know that. But I did lie. So show me the area in my heart that caused me to think that I need to lie, and help me to better understand how this problem works so I can find a solution and move past it.

So I ask myself, "Why did I feel the need to lie in this situation?" Oh! Because I was afraid this person would get mad at me if they knew the truth, and I didn't want to deal with the lecture as a consequence for the mistake I made. So right away I learn two new things that need improvement: 1) I don't trust this certain person and I'm afraid they will punish me for my mistakes. 2) I have a fear of taking responsibility for my actions because I don't want to face the consequences.

Since I've zeroed in on the source of the problem, I'm in a better position to change my mind about those things so I can see *real* improvement in that area of my life, instead of substituting improvement with spirituality that only keeps me running in circles. In changing my heart about those things, I eliminate the source of the problem, rather than merely covering it up and trying harder to resist it (or pretend it isn't there).

Since I feel safe around Him, I'm able to stick around and learn from Him, rather than running away to the shadows to hide.

There are still habits of self-condemnation that I'm learning to break, so I don't want to give anyone the impression that I have everything together. Since I spent so much of my life being upset at myself whenever I messed something up, I'm still learning how to renew my mind to be more gentle with myself. So even in things that aren't directly related to Christianity, when I mess something up, and I feel like someone is disappointed in me for messing up, I apologize to them, and I remind myself, "I'm new to this. I can't expect myself to be an expert at it right away, and neither can they." And while that accusing voice taunts me, "Wow! You can't do anything right! They're so mad at you!" I smile and tell myself again, "I've never done this before, but I'll get better at it." I don't work myself up and try to fight against that voice to prove how much faith I have (I've learned my lesson about that. It only leads to unnecessary exhaustion), instead I remain at rest and comfort myself with the truth I know about God and how He sees me.

In staying conscious of the fact that I'm a student, and therefore keeping myself in a humble position to learn, the burden of performance and stress of perfectionism is lifted. I'm able to continue approaching life as a humble student willing to learn and advance (and therefore willing to make mistakes), rather than living under the pressure that I need to act like a religious professor who knows everything and has it all together (where mistakes are often forbidden and looked down upon).

What Do You Believe About Yourself?

People may think I'm a great writer now, but when I first started writing, my work was practically unreadable! My writing was done in big blocks of text, all in a single paragraph, with no punctuation and numerous typos. It was a mess. But because I've been doing it constantly for so long, I've not only learned to do better through my own trial and error, making conscious decisions to change certain things, but by reading books and articles that show me how writing works, so I can put those things into practice and improve in this area.

Same thing with typing—I'm a mad man on the keyboard. But when I first started using a computer, I just used my index finger to poke the keys, while concentrating intensely on the keyboard. But after ten years of experience with a keyboard, it's first nature to know where the keys are, so I no longer even need to take my eyes off of the screen while I type, and I've learned to incorporate all of my other fingers (except my pinky) into typing.

I'm by no means an expert writer or typist, but I'm miles ahead of where I was when I began. But imagine if I had taken the approach that so many of us had taken with sin.

> "I'm always going to be a horrible writer and typist until I die! I'll never improve because it's just my nature to write bad! I'm prone to typos and bad punctuation!"

Had I believed that about myself, then you can bet I wouldn't have written an entire book from scratch in just under a month. I would have spent just that month typing the first paragraph, and the entire book itself would have been one very long paragraph filled with typos. But because I never believed that about myself (mostly due to the fact that nobody ever put that idea in my head), being a below-average writer for the rest of my life never even crossed my mind, which left the gates wide open for improvement.

On the other hand, I've been playing guitar for ten years. I'm left handed, and I learned on a right handed guitar, so the guitar is upside down. After these ten years, I'm probably still considered a beginner guitar player. I believed the idea that I can't ever truly be great guitar player since I don't play it the right way. Although I've still continued to play it, and have learned a few new chords here and there, I've never actually felt inspired to really sit down and intentionally try to push my skill to the next level, since I didn't think I could.

I've met many people who have only been playing guitar for a few years, and their skill is already light-years beyond mine. Why? Because they believe improvement is an ever-expanding universe, and I believed there was an eventual end (at least for me personally).

It's the same with sin. Even though we're given strict demands to improve, we're told that we never can improve because we're "prone to sin" and it's our nature to always sin until we die. In believing such a stupid lie, we let the gates close and limit our ability to actually move forward and get better! (I so hope this book will remove that perception from your mind forever. There are no limits, save for the ones in your mind that tell you there are. And this is where renewing your mind is put into practice. I'll get better at guitar as soon as I start believing I can.)

"Everything is possible for him who believes." "Nothing is impossible with God." We quote those verses all the time, but then make nonsense excuses for why some things just aren't possible. "Nobody can live sinless except Jesus!" Really? Show me that in scripture.

> "It's right here! Romans 3:23, 'All have sinned and fall short of the glory of God' Ha! Take that!"

Good one! But did you notice that there's a comma at the end of that verse? That means the sentence continues in the next verse. "...and all are justified freely by his grace through the redemption that came by Christ Jesus." The period isn't placed after we fall, but after we've been picked back up.

Only Jesus Can Do That!

The idea that only Jesus can live sinless comes from the idea that we must keep our humanity separate from His divinity for fear of offending such a holy God with our disgustingness. Meanwhile, it was His idea to merge His divinity with our humanity in the first place. He proved this by sending His son in the form of human flesh, and through that Son making Himself one in Spirit with those "disgusting" humans (that's you and I!).

In fact, there are no scriptures that say "only Jesus can do that!" Quite the opposite, Jesus said over and over again, "Anyone who believes in me will do what they've seen me do" (and greater). Now, we could say that He was *only* speaking of healing and miracles, however, I find it strange to believe that He's telling me I can bring a dead person back to life, but I could never live free from the desire to open a porno-mag.

"So you think you're God?"

No. But I'm His son. He lives in me, and I'm one spirit with Him. We're inseparable and indistinguishable, and it was His idea and His will that it should happen that way, not mine. I could have never thought of such a thing. That's what you will find in scripture, but nothing about how our humanity offends Him or how He wants to keep a clear separation between our humanity and His holiness.

"You're wrong! We can never be like Christ!"

So then why is every Christian's goal to be Christ-like? If I can never be like Christ, why am I told to try so hard to resemble Him? Is it the same hopeless endeavor like it is to struggle to avoid sin even though you know it's your nature to always sin?

"Try to be Christ-like! (But you can never be like Christ.)"

"Try to quit sinning! (But you're always going to sin.)"

What kind of good news is that?

The Ineffectiveness of Our Traditions

We have fallen for such cruel lies in the church, and then made ourselves believe that our humanity is the problem instead of realizing it's our mindsets and the things we've accepted as truth. But because they've come from the leaders in the church who are placed high atop pyramids and pedestals, and who often use their positions to pressure us into quietly *submitting to their authority* by not asking questions (outside of the religiously-appropriate ones they sanction), we just automatically assume that these traditions are true, and they work. After all, these are the way things have been done for years!

If we question the traditions of Christianity, we are questioning GOD! Meanwhile, it was Christ who said, "It's the traditions you pass down that make the word of God ineffective!"[1] Why? Because we place more value in our traditions than we do in the Word of God Himself. In Mark 7 He was addressing the very problem that God's own followers treated their traditions more important than God's own Word (to such an extent that they killed God's Word on a cross because He threatened their traditions).

You're not the problem, what you believe about yourself is. So how do we deal with this issue? Let's find out.

Endnotes

[1] See Mark 7:13

Know Who You Are

Imagine a cop with a badge and a gun who comes face to face with a criminal. All of the sudden the cop begins to believe that the criminal has more authority than him, so he lays down his gun and slowly stands up with his hands in the air. The criminal doesn't actually have any authority at all, but because the cop believes the criminal does he doesn't try to put the criminal in his place. From the criminal's perspective, he would be foolish not to take advantage of the situation, wouldn't he?

In the same way, the devil has no authority. But if he sees that a person with authority is willing to lay down their gun (out of fear, unbelief, or whatever the reason), he won't mind taking advantage of the situation and using their authority against them.

We can look at it like this: you have faith, the devil has none. What does faith do? It moves mountains. What does the devil do if he wants to move a mountain? He looks to deceive someone who has faith so he can get them to move the mountain for him (and perhaps even trick them into prophesying an earthquake or two and pointing the finger at God!). He will lie, cheat and deceive you until you throw that mountain into the sea, and then he will make you feel like the biggest idiot for letting it happen (or make you think it was God's will so you'll feel like a spiritual hero and do it again!).

"Look what you did!" He'll say. "You're not a real Christian! A real Christian would have never done that!"

"God, that's so true." You reply to what you think are your own thoughts. "A real Christian wouldn't have acted that way. What if I'm not a real Christian?"

"Yeah! What if you're not even saved and God sends you to hell? Look at how wicked you are!"

"Oh my goodness. What if God sends me to hell because I'm not really saved?"

He's merciless. But let me add a useful weapon to your arsenal.

Fearlessness

> *There is no fear in love. But perfect love drives out fear, because fear has to do with punishment. The one who fears is not made perfect in love. – 1 John 4:18 (NIV)*

Perfect love drives fear *out*, not in. Why? Because fear has to do with punishment. It's the idea that God, who is perfect love, is going to hurt or reject you if you fail to live up to a certain standard. The one who fears is not made perfect in love. Why? Because they have yet to understand just how perfectly He loves them. They still think He is slow to love and abounding in anger when scripture says He's slow to anger and abounding in love.[1]

He will never leave you. He will never forsake you. He will never treat you as your sins deserve. In fact, He has promised to never even be angry with you again![2]

So how do you get made perfect in love? Next verse.

We love because he first loved us. – 1 John 4:19 (NIV)

Love isn't a result of rigorous discipline and desperate attempts to live on God's good side. Love is the natural response of experiencing His love for you. Take a break from working so hard to show your love for God and let Him show His love for you. His love will drive out all fear of punishment, and next time that little snake tries to convince you that you're on your way to hell because of some sin you did, your reaction will be laughter, not fear.

You give the devil permission to harm you when you agree with the lies he tells you. It's not that he has any power, but if you fail to recognize the power you have, you won't hesitate to surrender your gun. You being a sinner who is prone to sin is one of the biggest lies he has convinced the church to accept as truth, and it's one of the major reasons sin still has such a huge hold on Christians.

Even though Christians invest so much energy into fighting sin, they simultaneously believe they're supposed to continue sinning because it's their nature and who they are. So no wonder the devil is so easily able to tempt people away into sin. Those people are only doing what they think is the natural thing to do! (Even though they say they shouldn't do it.)

"But we will always sin until we die!"

Well then, good news, my friend: *You already died*! Now you are alive to God in Christ.[3]

Actions vs. Identity

It's knowing who you are in Him and who He is in you that makes sin so much easier to deal with, because it removes the struggle that sounds like Romans 7—"I want to do good, but I'll never carry it out!"—and replaces it with a confidence in Christ that really believes, "I *can* do good because I was created in Christ to do good!"[4]

Usually people hear these things for the first time and ask in a snarky tone, "So you don't sin anymore?"

Yes. I do.

"So doesn't that make you a sinner?"

No. It doesn't.

My identity is forever established in Him. Who I am is now based on who He is—it's based on His works, not mine. The focus is on what He did, not on what I do. Why? So no one can boast.[5]

If who I am were based on what I do, then I can rub it in your face if I obey more rules than you. I would technically be more holy and righteous because holiness and righteousness is measured by whoever behaves the best. But since my actions don't give me my identity—His do—I can never brag about anything but what He has done, because the same thing that's available to me is available to every single human being on this planet, whenever they choose to trust in His work and stop trusting in their own.

If righteousness was gained by our good works and great obedience, Christ died for nothing. But it was through *His* good work and great obedience that righteousness came. He became sin that I might become the righteousness (the moral rightness) of God.[6] That's why Paul said, "If anyone boasts, let them boast in the Lord," because Jesus is the one who did it all for us. We can only boast in His work because our work and performance can never add to or take away from what He has already done.[7] I can never say I'm a better Christian than you because I have everything you have, and you have everything I have, no matter what either one of us have done or will do.

The difference is in who actually believes it, and who doesn't, because the one who believes it will naturally learn to live it out (emphasis on "learn"). Since my focus isn't on sin, I'm prone to sin less. I'm not trying not to sin, I'm learning how to be like Him. So my eyes are focused on the things above, not the things on earth. I'm keeping my eyes on Him and letting Him change the habits of my heart, rather than keeping my eyes on sin and thinking my heart is unchangeable until I die or He raptures me.

If I do become conscious of an action that goes against my nature in Him (a sin), I deal with it. But I'm not actively on a hunt for sin in my own life or anyone else's; I'm enjoying my freedom from that life, and now I exist to deliver that freedom to others.

Faith in Who?

We have two choices:

1. Refuse His work and continue in ours (also known as the Law of sin and death, and self-righteousness)[8], OR

2. Rest in His work and accept that we're already sanctified and holy, and we're already His righteousness.[9]

You're not a sinner who's prone to sin, you're a saint who's prone to righteousness because righteousness is who you are. You are God's moral rightness by definition. The you that *was* prone to sin is dead.[10] The reason you can't be a sinner (even if you sin) is because who you are is no longer based on what you do, it's based on what He did for you. When you were under the Law, it was entirely based on your performance, but under grace (where you are right now) it's entirely based on His.

We're not God's righteousness because we did something for it, and neither do we keep God's righteousness because we do anything to keep it. If we did nothing to receive it, we can do nothing to keep it or lose it. And if we could do anything to gain or keep this gift, then there was no need for Jesus. On the contrary, we're God's righteousness because He chose to make us that way through His own work, and we chose, through faith (confidence and trust in His work), to reap the reward of the harvest He sowed.

It's not just by grace you have been saved, it's by grace through faith.[11] That simply means that you put faith in what grace has already made available. And even though grace makes it available, faith is what makes it a reality that you will walk out—just like grace made salvation available, but faith is what makes the benefits of that salvation a reality in someone's life.

If I come into your room dangling keys and say, "I got you a brand new car downstairs!" My grace (kindness you didn't earn) has made that car available, but faith is what will make you get up and grab the keys. Why are you grabbing those keys? Because you trust me when I say, "I got you a new car!"

Faith in Jesus is no more complicated than that. I trust Him when He says I'm free, and it's faith in what He says that inspires me to stand up, receive His gift, and then enjoy it.

If you didn't trust me when I said I got you a brand new car, or you say, "No! I'm so unworthy of your gift!" then you'll just stay there in your bed, asking God to bless you with a brand new car, and you won't move anywhere... but that car will still be there.[12] Likewise, freedom is there whether anyone takes it or not. But nobody takes it unless someone first tells them that it's there, and that person believes the message and receives the gift.

How to Be Transformed

"Be transformed by the renewing of your mind." (Romans 12:2)

You don't get transformed by the effort of your prayers, or the length of your fasting, or the volume of your crying out, or how genuinely you sing in church, or how well you can avoid sin, or by how often you read, memorize, quote and preach the Bible, but only by renewing your mind—changing the way you think and learning to see things from a new perspective.[13]

If you're struggling with sin, change the way you think. Renew your mind—that's what repentance means. It doesn't mean you have to cry at an altar, it simply means to bring your mind into the new way of thinking. You're not the victim of sin, but the victor over it through Christ's finished work.

Freedom from sin starts by putting faith in His work and taking faith out of your own work (whether it's good or bad). You can never sin enough to be a sinner because sin can never taint the righteousness of God, which is who you are. He has forever perfected those who are being sanctified, and yet, you've already been sanctified by God's will through the offering of the body of Christ.[14]

Once again, it was *His* will and *His* offering, not *yours*.

If I happen to become aware of a sin (which is becoming increasingly more rare), I don't curl into the fetal position and cry about how sinful and stupid I am (I practically used to do that!). Instead I remind myself of what Jesus accomplished and how much He has set me free from those uncontrollable actions.

I keep His work (not my own) at the forefront of my mind, and I let His work (not my own) be the motivator in how I live my life. I'm not trying to avoid sin in order to impress God, I'm staying conscious of the fact that He is already impressed. And the more I understand this, the more sin is naturally avoided without me even having to try. Although I don't completely ignore sin (I personally like figuring out what influences certain behaviors so I can help myself and others), it isn't the primary focus.

Now, going back to faith, don't complicate it or let the thought of it intimidate you like it has for so many people for so long. Faith isn't this exhausting thing that you have to work up or pretend to have an enormous amount of around your Christian peers. We've made it into such a hassle! But like the car example above, faith simply means "If You said it, I believe it." What did Jesus say? "You're free indeed." Do you believe Him? Then get up and grab the keys!

Endnotes

[1] Neh. 9:16-18

[2] See Isa. 54:9

[3] See Rom. 6:10-11

[4] See Eph. 2:10

[5] See Eph. 2:8-10

[6] See 2 Cor. 5:21. Definition from Merriam-Webster.com.

[7] See 1 Cor. 1:30-31

[8] See 2 Cor. 3:7, Heb. 4

[9] See Heb. 4:10-11

[10] See Rom. 6:2, 6:7, 6:10-11, Gal. 5:24, Col. 2:11

[11] See Eph. 2:8-10

[12] "The gifts of God are irrevocable." (Romans 11:29)

[13] I'm obviously not against reading the Bible. My point is that many boast of how they've read through the entire Bible a few times, but their life still stinks and they're still stuck in horrible sins. It doesn't matter how much you read it if you're not doing anything with it. James said, "Don't merely listen to the word or you deceive yourselves. Do what it says." Put what you read into practice. "Consider yourselves dead to sin." What does that look like in practice? Next time you get a thought that says, "I'm such a sinner!" You say, "NO! I'm a saint. I'm holy, righteous and perfect in Christ. I am hidden in Him. I no longer live, Christ lives in me! So I talk about Him and His work, not mine!" The more you do it, the more natural it becomes because you are actually putting what you read to use.

[14] See Heb. 10:10

Getting Our Priorities in Order

In 2011, I worked at McDonalds, where my job consisted of standing at the drive-thru window for 8 hours, taking orders and collecting money from very sassy people who clearly hated their jobs as much as I did. About three months into the job, something strange began to happen while I was standing in the drive-thru. My mind became flooded with very detailed lustful thoughts about the women who pulled up to the window. We're talking full-HD, full-color pornographic projections, clearer than my own physical eyes can see—it was bizarre and uncomfortable to say the least.

I was established enough in my identity at this time to know that those kinds of thoughts weren't originating in my own heart or mind, so I didn't fall to my knees and pray, "Oh, God! Save me, I'm my own worst enemy!" like I would have before. I knew there was something else behind it, so I started resisting it and *trying* not to lust. I silently told those thoughts (and the devil behind them), "Jesus said, 'Don't lust,' so I'm not going to!" And, as always is the case with the Law, the harder I tried to obey it and use it as a weapon against sin and temptation, the worse the problem became ("The strength of sin is the Law").

This happened for a few days, each day becoming more frustrating than the last. Finally I got a bright idea to talk to my Father about the problem. I said, "What the heck, God? I don't know why this is happening. I know it's not me and I know you said, 'Don't lust,' but I don't know how to stop these thoughts, and they're annoying! Why could I so easily get rid of these thoughts before, but now they're not going away?"

Within seconds He answered me, "You were valuing the person before, now you're valuing the command, 'Do not lust.' Why did Jesus say, 'Do not Lust'?"

It was another one of those questions I had somehow failed to ask through my entire Christian life. "Why *did* Jesus say that?" I stood there contemplating this question, and almost immediately I began to understand. Lust distorts and damages how we relate to people, and *that* is the overall problem God has with sin as a whole. God's issue with sin isn't as pathetic as "You broke my rules!" His issue is that sin causes us to relate to Him, ourselves and other people in a way that we were never created to. It drives a divide between you and the person created to be your companion (whether romantically or platonically). As we talked about in chapter 6, it corrupts our perception of God and humanity.

For the Bible Tells Me So

When I had dealt with these same problems before, I did so easily because I learned to value the person above the command—grace taught me to see people instead of rules. However, when I was struggling with these thoughts in the drive-thru, since my usual tactic didn't work right away, I began to panic and aimlessly quote scripture about not doing the thing I knew the Bible told me not to do. In doing so, I began valuing the command over the people. I was ritualistically trying to make these things go away with the command, oblivious to the reason the command was given in the first place.

As I stood there in the drive-thru with a huge grin on my face, trying to keep the giggling to a minimum over this new life-changing revelation I received, I began to examine the Ten Commandments and *why* they were given.

"Do not lie."

Why? Because when I lie, I damage the trust in a relationship which causes separation between me and the other person.

"Do not commit adultery!"

Why? Because once again, I betray the trust in the relationship and I cause a separation between me and the other person.

As I went through each one, I found that similarity over and over again. The point of the Law wasn't that we would idolize the rules and try our hardest to keep them, but that we would better understand how God wants to protect relationships, just as "do not eat from this tree" wasn't an arbitrary rule, but it was meant to protect the Creation. That's what Jesus said the sum of the Law is: to love your neighbor, yourself, and God. It's not merely about keeping rules, it's about the reason behind the rules, which always comes back to love.

Oftentimes today we think the most faithful thing we can do is not ask questions and just go along with anything we're told. I've often asked questions on my Facebook page about why we in the church do certain things, and I've had numerous people respond by saying, "Because the Bible says so!" or "Because God said so! Why are you questioning God?"

"Because the Bible said so!" is one of the most destructive reasons to obey what the Bible says. It gives you absolutely no guidance or room to learn and grow in knowledge. You never have the opportunity to learn how things work, or why they work the way they do, you're just constantly in robot mode—"God said push this button, so I better push this button." Why did He say push the button? What does the button do? Why does the button do that? How does pushing the button cause the reaction it causes? Why is that reaction important? That probably sounds annoying to some of you. But that's how I think. I want to know how things work and why they work the way they do, because I want to know if there's any way to improve. I'm not content with "This is the way it is and you better just go with it!" No. Is there a better way to do this? Can we be more efficient about it? Can we get more done with less work?

Many people just want to "obey." But the person who never asks questions is never empowered to obey anything at all because they never encounter the heart of the person who gave the command in the first place, so they never understand the heart in which those commands were given. They aren't listening to God, but instead they are listening to words carved into dead stones.

See, what happens when people only go by the words of the command without engaging in true relationship with the person who gave them the command is that they elevate the command above the Person. That's where sin seizes the opportunity to make the issue worse, by using man's zeal to obey the command against him.

Many will proudly proclaim that they are in a relationship with Jesus, but how many other relationships are you in where you're scared to ask questions? How many are you in where you just feel the pressure to do what you're told without knowing the reason why you're being told? Or even thinking you're not *allowed* to know why you're told.

If I'm not allowed to question the person I'm told to follow then it's not a relationship, it's a dictatorship. God is not a dictator expecting blind obedience; if you have a question, He is the Answer.

Am I being a Law preacher? No. I'm being a "heart-behind-the-Law" preacher. I'm telling you that God didn't just give commands to give commands, looking for blind obedience and thinking that's a sign of "faith." He gave commands with a specific purpose in mind (a few purposes, in fact). If you only try to obey the commands "because the Bible says!" then you're going to have a hell of a time with your Christianity, because you have absolutely no idea *why* the Bible says, which means you're only swinging blindly at the wind, unsure of what you're even aiming for.

Ask questions. Find out *why* these things were said. And I'll tell you right now, that when you go the route of asking questions, you'll have to deal with a lot of really mean Christians who will accuse you of being faithless for not just blindly going along with everything God says without asking questions. Some will be in high positions and will use their authority to intimidate you back into blind obedience to the Law and their interpretation of scripture. **Do not give in to them**. Those kinds of people have so spiritualized their blindness that it has become a point of pride.

The Laws were not meant to replace the golden calf; God never intended for those stone tablets to become an idol. They were meant to point those people to God, despite the fact that they were trying to get away from Him. Those people, even up into Jesus' day, idolized the Law. Take a good look at how that turned out for them, and learn from their mistake.

The Problem With Lust

Now, if I lust after a girl, I'm thinking of her in a way that she's not meant to be thought of: as an object that only serves to satisfy myself. It's not the desire for sex that's bad, it's when that desire gets hijacked and turned into a selfish desire that causes you to consider yourself better than the other person.

See, the beauty of a love relationship is that my primary concern is to look after the other person. But if fear creeps in, it tries to convince me that if I look out for them instead of myself, then who will look out for me? When we accept that fear, it causes us to want to look after ourselves to make sure we are taken care of first. However, in a legitimate relationship (not corrupted by fear and selfishness), each person looks out for the other (because "love is not self-seeking"). Consequently, both are taken care of equally without having to worry about taking care of themselves. This is the wonderful design of love. If two people in love seek the benefit of the other, both are taken care of, and have no fear that they won't be taken care of because there is trust. Since neither person has a "me, me, me" attitude, and both have a "you, you, you" attitude, both are cared for.

It's beautiful, isn't it?

Now the problem with lust is that it's all about me feeling good and finding pleasure for myself, with no concern for the other person at all. Although only in my mind to begin with, those thoughts portray the person far below their true value (not as a pearl to be cherished, but as one to be pawned off for personal gain). Where does the problem go if not dealt with in your mind? To your heart. Remember that Jesus never said lust is in your mind, but in your heart. It's not the thoughts that are the sin, it's the acceptance of those thoughts that leads to selfishness. All the pornographic thoughts in the world could pop into my mind, but until I take one of those thoughts and willingly and consciously step into that fantasy land where this person is treated as less than what they are worthy of, I'm not in the sin that Jesus spoke of. We can't help every thought that pops into our head, but we can make sure we take every thought captive and make it obedient to Christ. And you have the mind of Christ, so don't settle for the thinking that you have to think anything less than what He thinks.

So then are you free to think lustful thoughts as long as you don't "claim" them as your own? I'll let Paul answer that one.

> "I have the right to do anything," you say--but not everything is beneficial. "I have the right to do anything"--but not everything is constructive. No one should seek their own good, but the good of others." – 1 Cor. 10:24 (NIV)

I've tried to experiment and see how long I could think about the female body before it turned into lust, and I even went looking up nude pictures on the internet with the mindset, "I'm looking with an appreciation for the female body, not with the intention of sexualizing these women." It worked for a bit. But within the next few days those images I saw would come back really strong in my mind, stir up desires, and then distort those desires into lust. Although those pictures didn't bother me at the time—and I was even able to look at them with innocence—those images remained in my subconscious mind where the enemy often tries to attack. I pretty much handed him a box of ammunition and said, "Fire away!" I've found it better to guard my heart and my mind so he has nothing to fire at me at a later time. Therefore, the conclusion for me (and feel free to learn from my mistakes so you don't have to make them yourself) is that there is no benefit in trying to walk that line. I've found it better to stay on the safe side and keep my mind clear of those things, rather than give him one more thought to twist and use against me.

Rituals

Now, I was standing in the drive-thru, incredibly excited to be learning all of these practical answers. I knew that next time one of those thoughts popped into my head, instead of trying to convince myself, "Jesus said not to lust! So I'm not going to!" I would say to the thoughts and whatever was behind them, "No. She's more valuable than that and I won't think of her as less than what she's worth." What happened when I did that? *Poof!* The thoughts didn't get worse, they disappeared altogether. I felt instant clarity in my mind and a relief from the frustration of the previous three days. Since I had just become established in Truth based on love (value for the other person instead of the rule), the attempts at getting me to accept these selfish thoughts lost their foothold.

Now, this is a very important part to pay attention to. I'm not telling you these things to give you a method, a formula, or a new phrase to chant in order to get rid of lustful thoughts. As I've had to learn the hard way many times, trying to turn these kinds of successes into some kind of religious formula or method quickly zaps the power right out of them, because the faith is withdrawn from the Person and placed in the method. So I'm telling you these things to show you how important it is to find out the *reason* you are told to do (or not do) something. Stay in constant communion with Him and never be afraid to ask Him the hard questions.

It's the answer to the "why" question that will empower you. Simply going by, "Jesus said..." or "The Bible says..." actually made the problem I was dealing with worse. But when I found out *why* Jesus said so (to teach me to value others, not the rule), I was provided with the solution to the problem. I was able to "change my mind" (repent) and look at the person as He looks at them, instead of disregarding the person for the sake of the rule, and trying my hardest to keep it.

My heart wasn't to avoid lust because of an abstract command, but to avoid it because I found genuine value in the person those thoughts sought to destroy. In love, selfishness is immediately disarmed and destroyed.

So am I recanting on what I said earlier in the book about living free from the Law? No. Because the curse of the Law is that as long as one tries to keep the Law, they will continue to break it. It wasn't the Law that helped me on that day in the drive-thru (trying to obey the Law actually made everything worse), but it was the grace of the person who gave the Law (and understanding the reason He gave the Law) that helped me. It was letting the shadow lead me to the reality of the person that set me free.

The Law is holy, righteous and good when it points us to Jesus, as it's intended to do. But when it points us to ourselves, and fuels the self-righteous determination to obey the rule apart from the Person, then it becomes death to us. I'm not saying to try and live up to the Law, I'm saying that if you're going to give the Law any attention at all, let it do what it was created to do, which is point you to the person of Christ. He must always be the conclusion to everything written in scripture, otherwise scripture fails to live up to its purpose.[1]

You can try to keep as many rules as you'd like, but if the dead stones never lead you to the living person, it matters not.

Endnotes

[1] See John 5:39

Common Questions and Concerns

"Aren't we all sinners saved by grace?"

Despite this being a very popular quote among Christians in the church today, it's not actually accurate. The saying that we are "sinners saved by grace" is a man-modified version of Eph. 2:8 which says that "we are saved by grace, not by works."

"Sinners saved by grace" is a popular misquote, and because it has been quoted this way so often for so long many say it as if it's actually in scripture. But neither Jesus nor Paul ever referred to anyone in the church as being "sinners." In fact, they often referred to them as the exact opposite!

Paul began every letter to his churches with "to the saints..." not "to the sinners..." Even when he was correcting their sinful behavior, he continued to reassure them of who they were in Christ, and he never let their actions become the thing by which they were identified, or be an excuse to belittle them. He always made sure to point their identity back to Jesus and the benefits they shared in Him.

Likewise, Jesus told His disciples, "You are already clean because of the word I have spoken to you."[1] He didn't reassure them of their filthiness, but of their cleanliness because they were identified together with Him.

"Doesn't scripture say 'no one is righteous'?"

Yes. The verse is in Romans 3, but Paul is quoting Psalms 14. The thing to understand about Paul is that oftentimes when he was quoting verses from the Old Testament, it was because he was setting up a contrast between then and now. Just as Jesus did when He said, "You have heard it said... but I say to you," Paul was giving them an update between the time of the Old, and the time of the New.

Now when Paul says that no one is righteous, he is speaking in the context of those under the law. Look at the verses directly following the quote from the Psalmist.

> *"Now we know that whatever the law says it speaks to those who are under the law, so that every mouth may be stopped, and the whole world may be held accountable to God. For by works of the law no human being will be justified in his sight, since through the law comes knowledge of sin." –*
> *Romans 3:19-20 (ERV)*

He's talking about no one being righteous under the Law. Which we can all agree on, since scripture says over and over that nobody is justified or made righteous by the Law. But Paul doesn't just stop at the "no one is righteous" bad news like many do. Read on and look what he says.

> *"**But now** the righteousness of God has been manifested apart from the law, although the Law and the Prophets bear witness to it— the righteousness of God through faith in Jesus Christ for all who believe." – Romans 3:21 (NIV)*

What is he saying?

- The bad news: "Yes, under the law not a single person is righteous; neither can anyone ever be made righteous under the law!"
- The Good news: "**But now** the righteousness of God has been manifested (presented) apart from the law, through faith in Christ. There is no distinction between Greek and Jew, for all [under the law] fall short of the glory of God, and [apart from the law] are justified by his grace as a gift... through Jesus... to be received by faith."

If we're to believe the section that says, "None are righteous," then we have to accept the rest of the verse which includes, "no one seeks God." And if no one seeks God, then that proposes a big problem for the many popular ministries and prayers that zealously declare how much they are seeking God!

"God, we just seek you, tonight!"

No you don't. Not if no one is righteous! Because if no one is righteous, then no one seeks God. Not only that, but we're all worthless. So are we to believe all of the verse, or just the one line that makes us feel secure in our belief that we're sinners?

Paul is speaking in the context of being under the Law (that seems to be a common theme throughout Romans, doesn't it?). Therefore, we have to view these verses in that context, and also with the understanding that he is building up to a bigger point, where he will tell them, "We are no longer under law, but under grace!" and then go into how we have been set free from sin and every effect of sin that have plagued humanity for so long.

He's not simply saying, "no one is righteous" just to be saying it. He's leading them to an eventual outcome of good news. And he is doing so by contrasting that good news with bad news so that we will *really* understand how good this news is.

We also have to remember that this is the same guy who told the Corinthians, "you have become the righteousness of God." (1 Cor. 5:21)

"Didn't Paul call himself the 'worst of sinners'?"

This one phrase has messed up the lives of so many people! Coincidentally, I'm in the middle of writing a book about this section of scripture. Yes, Paul called *himself* the worst of sinners, but note that he never called you or anybody else that. And to understand why he even said this in the first place, do you know what we have to do? That's right! We have to look at the context of the verses.

To sum it up, Paul is writing this letter (1 Timothy) to command Timothy to confront some teachers of the Law. Now while he is giving Timothy these instructions he begins to give his testimony. In verses 12-17 of 1 Timothy 1, Paul is telling Timothy how he used to be a blasphemer and a violent man, and how he used to persecute the church in the name of God. Then he tells Timothy of how God had shown him mercy despite those horrible things, because he did those things in ignorance and unbelief.

Did God pour out his wrath on Paul or destroy a nearby city with an earthquake? No. Instead Paul says God poured out His grace in abundance, along with the faith and love that are in Christ Jesus. Paul, despite his mercilessness, received mercy from God, and this is the same mercy that changed his heart forever.

Now, during his testimony is when he includes the "trustworthy saying" bit that so many have taken out of context.

> *"Here is a trustworthy saying that deserves full acceptance: Christ Jesus came into the world to save sinners—of whom I am the worst." (NIV)*

The trustworthy saying doesn't include the "worst of sinners" part. You can see the em dash there (—) which indicates that it's a secondary thought (some translations like the NLT, use quotations marks that make this easier to see). The trustworthy saying is only meant to be "Christ Jesus came into the world to save sinners." Period. The "worst of sinners" part is only a secondary thought added in by Paul, referencing the testimony he had just given Timothy about how he had done all of those horrible things.

Why is he calling himself the worst of sinners? Not as a display of spiritual humility, but to emphasize the grace and mercy God showed him, and wants to show everyone else. Why does he think this is important? Because he is sending Timothy to confront these teachers of the Law. And what did Paul used to be? A teacher of the Law. These people he is sending Timothy to confront are just like Paul used to be—they think they are doing God's work, but they are steeped in ignorance and unbelief.

If you read the context of the letter, while Paul is telling Timothy to confront these people and command them to stop speaking of things they know nothing about, he is also making it clear that Timothy should do so with gentleness and love. So in giving Timothy his testimony and saying, "I'm the worst of sinners, but God had mercy on me," he is emphasizing God's desire to have mercy, not only on these Law teachers, but on everyone.

"But for that very reason I was shown mercy so that in me, the worst of sinners, Christ Jesus might display his immense patience as an example for those who would believe in him and receive eternal life." (1:16)

Paul wasn't calling himself the worst of sinners as a show of spiritual humility, like so many think they are doing today when they quote this phrase. He was doing so to reinforce God's abounding grace towards sinners—even the worst. By saying, "God has had mercy on the worst," he is saying that there is nobody who God will not have mercy on, not even these law teachers Timothy is being told to confront. It was for this very reason that God had mercy on him, so that through him the whole world would see His immense patience for sinners—even the worst.

He wasn't giving Christians permission to take that phrase and apply it to themselves, because he was never talking about them in the first place! He was talking about himself in the context of his old life before he was a Christian. Because what is a testimony? It's the story of how you *used to be*, compared to how you are now after receiving Jesus.

Don't we have to Die Daily?

No. Romans 6 says you died "once for all" with Christ. How do you kill someone every day who has died once and never came back from the grave? Unless you get a kick out of trying to kill dead men, there's really no point in wasting your energy on this. It's like shadow boxing and hoping to win a trophy.

The three words used to fuel this belief actually come from a part in scripture that has nothing to do with sin at all. *Surprise!*

In the King James Version (and a few others) of 1 Cor. 15:31, Paul uses the phrase, "I die daily." Somehow this got ripped out of context and used to coerce people into thinking they need to continuously get rid of their sinful selves every day. Thankfully, other Bible versions have translated it more accurately to say, "I face death daily," because the context in which Paul used those words is in telling the Corinthian church how much suffering and danger he has faced for the sake of the Gospel. He's saying this to counter the idea that there is no resurrection.

It has nothing to do with "crucifying your flesh daily," or dying daily. You already died, and you were raised to new life with Christ.

You don't need to worry about that old life anymore, or run back and try to tie up loose ends. Jesus already took care of it!

Now, in the sense of "putting off the old and putting on the new," there is a sense of killing old habits, or at least reminding yourself that the old flesh is already dead so you quit living as if it's still alive. This is what Paul deals with in Colossians 3 when he tells them to put off the old and put on the new. Is he telling them they need to strive to kill their sinful flesh? No. verse 11 says that old flesh has been killed. But as we talked about earlier in the book, there are still habits that need to be put off so you can live according to the new self. It's not about you striving to kill sin, it's about believing that it's already dead, and living accordingly.

"I still think we are sinners!"

That's fine. But it doesn't change the fact that scripture says you're holy (Heb. 10:10), righteous (2 Cor. 5:21), and perfect (Heb. 10:14). The point of this book is not to coerce or corral you into my belief system, but to give you an optimistic perspective that encourages you to stop judging yourself by the flesh (what you do), and start judging yourself by what He has done for you.

> "For the love of Christ controls us, because we have concluded this: that one has died for all, therefore all have died; and he died for all, that those who live might no longer live for themselves but for him who for their sake died and was raised.
>
> From now on, therefore, we regard no one according to the flesh. Even though we once regarded Christ according to the flesh, we regard him thus no longer. Therefore, if anyone is in Christ, he is a new creation. The old has passed away; behold, the new has come." – 2 Cor. 5:14-18 (ERV)

You're free to believe whatever you choose, but the Truth of this gospel, which I make no apologies about, is that you are a new person and the old one is gone. If you want to live like the new person, you must first believe that the old one is gone, otherwise you will continue struggling back and forth with a dead man. Should you get this overnight? I hope so! But it has been a process for me. I'm still learning, but I'm miles ahead of where I began, and light-years ahead of where I was when I just believed I was doomed and damned to live like a sinner every day.

It starts with believing this gospel, and then acting on it. If you merely read the words of this book and think, "Wow. That's good!" But you never do anything with what you hear, you deceive yourself. James said, "Do not just listen to the word, do what it says, or you deceive yourselves."

I could read a thousand books on playing guitar, but improvement doesn't start until I pick up a guitar and put what I've learned into practice. And even with a thousand books of head knowledge, I still have to train my fingers, my hand-eye coordination, my endurance, and much more. Even with a thousand books of head knowledge, I still have to practice and build my body for that purpose. But I'll be able to learn faster because of what I already know. And this is the point of the book, that I would give you a starting point.

Doesn't Scripture say, "The heart is deceitfully wicked..." (Jeremiah 17:9)?

Indeed it does! But then it says,

> *"I will give them a heart to know Me..." - Jeremiah 24:7 (NIV)*

And,

> *I will give you a new heart and put a new spirit in you; I will remove from you your heart of stone and give you a heart of flesh.- Ezekiel 36:26 (NIV)*

Or,

> *"I will also put a new spirit in you to change your way of thinking. I will take out the heart of stone from your body and give you a tender, human heart." (ERV)*

As Paul confirmed in 2 Cor. 5:17,

> *"Therefore, if anyone is in Christ, the new creation has come: The old has gone, the new is here!" (NIV)*

"Is this that new 'hyper grace' deception?"

Much of what I've written here might easily be lumped into a new category of slander called "hyper-grace." This term is often used negatively to imply that people are telling others it's okay to sin and do whatever they want. If you're interested in hearing the *truth* about what "hyper-grace" teachers believe, I've written a book called *Hyper-Grace: The Dangerous Doctrine of a Happy God*, where I clear up the many misconceptions and false accusations.

Endnotes

[1] See John 15:3

Acknowledgements

Shandy Pekkonen — you have forever ruined my life with the Gospel of grace and freedom. You've probably saved my life as well. I could thank you in every book I write, but no amount of eloquent words can ever truly express how thankful I am for what you've given me. For 6 years I struggled to "get back" to God the way I was when I first became a Christian, only to find out that I had never left Him, and He had never left me. Your words, your heart and your example ended my hopeless pursuit of pleasing God, and gave me the life-changing perspective that He is already pleased with me—not because I *do*, but because I *am*.

Kris Vallotton — I've still never met you, but you are one of my favorite people. I read your Facebook posts and I feel like we would be great friends. In 2006 I downloaded a 3-part podcast of yours called "Living in Graceland." Although I had no comprehension of its implications at the time, it's still my first memory of anyone ever implying that we can truly live free from sin in this life. I've experienced the anger, frustration and abandonment that comes when you say that kind of thing in public, and I'm sure you've experienced those things as well (seems to be the nature of the message), so thank you for enduring hate and cruelty to bring the world such a wonderful message of hope and freedom.

The Steckels — thank you for offering me a place of peace and quiet from which to pursue my passion without the pressures of life. For the short time I've known you all personally, I've learned so much about what it means to be family, and to truly live a life revolving around Jesus. You all are the real deal. I'm happy you are a part of my life, and I thank you for letting me be a part of yours!

My Facebook Page — to those who have shown me such great mercy and patience as I grow and learn—thank you. To those who have dared to publicly question my posts and get me thinking about what I say and believe—thank you. To those who have attacked me, accused me, or condemned me to hell for my posts—thank you (I've probably learned the most from you!).

A very special thanks to Joshua Greeson, Rebecca Clayton, Sarah Dunsworth and Paul Ellis for going the extra mile and pointing out typos and other grammatical errors. And to April Sherlock, Danae Copeland, Steven Yang, Darren Slone, Jayshawn Campbell, Corey Semeniuk, and the wonderful folks of /r/Christianity, for helping me put together the "Common Questions and Concerns" section of the book. I hope it (along with the rest of this book) serves its purpose well.

Other Books by D. R. Silva

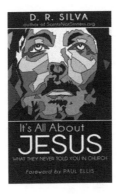

It's All About Jesus:
What They Never Told You in Church
(Available in Kindle and Paperback Format)

D. R. Silva challenges the biggest giants of modern church doctrine to see if they measure up next to the life of Jesus. This book will reveal the source of most problems in the Christian life and will show you how to find the quickest solution.

Is it God's will to heal everyone? Are you destined to sin until you die? Was Jesus sacrifice only for forgiveness of sins and heaven when you die? This book looks past all of the superficial catch phrases, spiritual hype, and countless excuses that have kept Christians powerless for years. It examines every question in the light of the life of Jesus, and the answers you find will shock and amaze you!

What People are Saying

"D. R. Silva's book, *It's All About Jesus*, is one of several refreshingly honest Christian books I've read lately. He is open about the process he's gone through in transitioning from what much of modern Christianity teaches, to a more authentic relationship with God in Christ." – **Joshua Greeson**, author of *God's Will is Always*

Healing

"This book will help those who are newer to the faith avoid some of the pitfalls the rest of us went through in the Christian walk." – **Steve Bremner**, SteveBremner.com

"I wish more people would ask the sorts of questions D. R. Silva raises in this book for they are questions that illuminate and liberate. And they are questions that will lead you to a deeper revelation of the greatest Answer of all." – **Paul Ellis**, author of *The Gospel in*

Twenty Questions, EscapeToReality.org

"This book was almost impossible to put down. If you have been on the spiritual "treadmill" looking for some answers, this is the book for you." – **Amazon Reviewer**

"If you are burned out trying to be 'good enough' for God, this book will help you find rest." – **Amazon Reviewer**

Hyper-Grace:
The Dangerous Doctrine of a Happy God
(Available in Kindle and Paperback Format)

- Are people really being told it's okay to sin and live immoral lives because we have grace?
- Do "hyper-grace" teachers say repentance and confession are unnecessary?
- Do "hyper-grace" teachers hate the Law?
- Are they ignoring the words of Jesus, or actually taking them seriously?
- Has God only forgiven your past sins, but left everything else up to you?

D. R. Silva once again challenges the giants of Christian tradition, this time correcting the popular assumptions, misconceptions and false accusations brought against "the modern grace message."

In this short and practical book, you will learn the foundational teachings of what has been deemed "hyper-grace." You will see that the "hyper-grace" teachings being opposed today are actually Biblical concepts found in scripture, and that it's the same Gospel Paul shamelessly preached, defended and died for.

What People are Saying

"I think every Christian should read this book." — **Amazon Reviewer**

"A book that will awaken your hope and wonder at God's grace and love for us." — **Amazon Reviewer**

"One of the best presentations on grace I have read." — **Amazon Reviewer**

"D. R. Silva has done a wonderful job explaining many of the objections people have against the Grace Movement happening today." — **Amazon Reviewer**

"After having been confused over what 'grace' is or isn't...this book made understanding and embracing God in all His grace easy." — **Amazon Reviewer**

ABOUT THE AUTHOR

D. R. Silva is a Best Selling author and compulsive question asker. His blog, SaintsNotSinners.org, has inspired tens of thousands of people around the world. Together, his highly acclaimed books, *It's All About Jesus: What They Never Told You in Church* and *Hyper-Grace: The Dangerous Doctrine of a Happy God* have helped set countless people free from bondage to legalistic religion. He is best known for his conversational writing style and frequent use of parables that make complex topics easy to understand. The goal of all of His writing is to point everything to Jesus.

Made in the USA
Middletown, DE
30 September 2015